OPPORTUNITIES

in

Writing
Careers

W9-BWL-210

OPPORTUNITIES

in

Writing
Careers

REVISED EDITION

ELIZABETH FOOTE-SMITH

McGraw·Hill

New York   Chicago   San Francisco   Lisbon   London   Madrid   Mexico City
Milan   New Delhi   San Juan   Seoul   Singapore   Sydney   Toronto

The *McGraw·Hill* Companies

Library of Congress Cataloging-in-Publication Data

Foote-Smith, Elizabeth.
    Opportunities in writing careers / by Elizabeth Foote-Smith. — Rev. ed.
        p.   cm.
    ISBN 0-07-145872-7 (alk. paper)
    1. Authorship—Vocational guidance.   I. Title.

    PN153.F66   2006
    808'.02'023—dc22   2005023102

1 2 3 4 5 6 7 8 9 0   DOC/DOC   0 9 8 7 6

ISBN 0-07-145872-7

Interior design by Rattray Design

McGraw-Hill books are available at special quantity discounts to use as premiums and sales promotions, or for use in corporate training programs. For more information, please write to the Director of Special Sales, Professional Publishing, McGraw-Hill, Two Penn Plaza, New York, NY 10121-2298. Or contact your local bookstore.

This book is printed on acid-free paper.

To Carol, Timothy, Christy, Adrienne,
Larissa, Heather, and Hana

Contents

Foreword

From writing restaurant reviews for your local paper to writing Pulitzer prize–winning novels, the career opportunities and options for writers are vast. As someone who has always had a love for language—my first job, at around age seven, was as the neighborhood storyteller, seated on an upturned fruit crate under the elm tree in my parents' front yard—I am here to attest to the myriad ways you can make a living by writing.

For example, if you are moved to fight for justice, you will want to read about opportunities in the field of journalism—both in print and online. It is here where individuals such as yourself dig deeper, ask the hard questions, consider all sides of every story, and strive to bring the truth to light, hoping to build a more honest, ethical world.

If you have an appreciation for accuracy in the minutest details, you will want to explore the professional opportunities in the specialized fields of legal, technical, and scientific writing. Here, you will be working with cutting-edge developments in these critically important areas.

Of course, many of you dream of writing the next Great American Novel, becoming an acclaimed poet, or writing the screenplay for next summer's blockbuster movie. Excelling in these fiercely competitive, creative careers takes more than innate talent: it demands education, feedback, development, and practice. Most of all, succeeding in these areas requires your consistent determination and a sustained commitment to realizing your dreams.

Do you have what it takes? To answer that honestly, you need to understand what the career of your dreams looks like in reality—when you wake up, get yourself to your workplace (be it an office, a kitchen table, a laptop computer, or a notepad), and pursue that dream every working day. In *Opportunities in Writing Careers*, you'll find essential, firsthand information from professional writers in a wide variety of careers—from a magazine editor to a romance novelist to a restaurant critic. Although their work is diverse, they share the dream of being a writer, and they have lived that dream through smooth sailing and rough waters; through fun, exciting projects and through assignments they may have felt would never end. You'll see the world of professional writing through their eyes, gain the insight you'll need to get yourself started, and be ready to go out there and make your own dreams a reality.

Good luck—now get going!

Elizabeth L. Lane
Director, Lane Editorial

OPPORTUNITIES

in

Writing
Careers

1

Writing Careers 101

You must keep sending work out; you must never let a manuscript do nothing but eat its head off in a drawer. You send that work out again and again, while you're working on another one. If you have talent, you will receive some measure of success—but only if you persist.

—Isaac Asimov

WITH TODAY'S MODERN technology, you need to be able to express yourself using the written word. No longer are you always able to communicate face to face. To survive in our world, you need to be able to write. Writing is more than just making marks on a page. Writing is forming letters. Letters are symbols, and each letter represents a sound of speech. Do you realize that words are also symbols? Words represent ideas, and we use these ideas to communicate our unique thoughts to others through e-mail messages, faxes, letters, and even written reports.

However, if you are reading this book, you are planning to take your writing skills much further than just personal communication. You are anticipating using your writing skills to earn a living. So this book is definitely for you. As you read each chapter, you will be able to examine how your own unique writing skills can earn you money.

Whether you choose to be a freelance writer or a salaried writer, this book is designed to provide basic information that you will need to make your decision. It approaches job descriptions, job opportunities, earnings, and salaries from a realistic point of view. It includes profiles of interesting people at various stages in their writing careers. The book will help you take a look at yourself and estimate your personal potential as a writer in many different areas.

In the next chapter, you will learn to assess yourself as a writer and maybe even find out why you want to write. Chapter 3 will give you helpful hints on getting started. Then, in Chapter 4, you will learn about freelance writing. Chapters 5 through 14 will give you an overview of different types of writing and help you decide which you are attracted to and which you would be best at. For example, do you want to write a poem, a short story, an article, or a novel? Or, do you want to write for a magazine or newspaper? Finally, the last chapter will give you advice about marketing your writing and getting started in the publishing industry.

No matter what type of writing you decide to do, you will have to meet monthly or daily deadlines. Reading this book will open your mind to different areas where you can get started with your writing career.

As a writer, you are trying to express and interpret ideas and facts in written form, but did you realize that right now you already share something with professional writers? Do you find that hard to believe? Well, it is not! Whether they are newspaper reporters, magazine writers, editors, scriptwriters, book authors, or advertising copywriters, they all have a common passion for the written word. You would not be reading this book if you did not share this passion. You are eager to get your words down, and you are looking for career opportunities that will enable you to use your love of words to make a living. As your career gets started, you probably will also share other writers' complaints about editors, guidelines, limitations, and deadlines. But you will be driven by the challenges of forming words into sentences and sentences into paragraphs and by your ability to communicate with the past and the future.

A writer should have another lifetime to see whether he is appreciated.

—Jorge Luis Borges

Just think. Today, more than two hundred years after his death, Voltaire (just one example of so many wonderful writers!) is still able to communicate whenever someone takes a volume of his work off the library shelf. That could be you two hundred years from now, still communicating with future generations. As a writer, you will become part of the process of transferring one generation to the next. Your work will stretch back as far as you know and forward even further than any of us can imagine.

The best way to become a writer is to write. Just get started. The more you write the better a writer you will become. According to David Wright, former editor of the *Chicago Tribune*, it does not matter what you are writing; the practice will help make your writing faster, tighter, better, and more original. But you must be willing to try.

As you read this book, remember that every author whose work you enjoy was once a first-time writer like you. However, not everyone reading this book will get published. Those who are willing to research, be prepared, and, most important, be persistent in their efforts to pursue a writing career will be among the successful. Get started reading this book now, so that you will be able to pursue your dream of a writing career.

2

Why Do You Want to Write?

The act of writing is the act of discovering what you believe.
—David Hare

WRITERS ARE MOTIVATED to write for a wide variety of reasons: to express themselves, to inform, to entertain, and to influence. Others write for the gratification that comes with fame or money. Joyce Christmas, author of eleven mysteries, says she is motivated to write because she likes to finish what she is working on. Joyce adds that money is a factor, too, meaning that as a professional writer, writing is a job. Now, look at the following survey items and see what motivates you to write. Rank your choices in the order that is most important to you. Put the number one next to your first choice and then continue until you have made your selections.

Strong role model
Teacher

Accidental motivation
Fame
Financial opportunities
Literature: reading a particular body of work
Need to write
Not wanting to work nine to five
Wanting to be part of the literary community

This survey was conducted by the world association of Playwrights, Essayists, Editors, and Novelists (known as PEN). Now compare your results and see if you are motivated by the same top choices that motivate other writers.

Need to write	282
Literature: reading a particular body of work	212
Teacher	99
Fame	76
Wanting to be part of the literary community	72
Not wanting to work nine to five	55
Strong role model	49
Accidental motivation	24
Financial opportunities	17

As a career, writing provides the writer with a wide range of personal satisfaction. Writing offers the writer the opportunity to learn not only about the external world, but also, and perhaps even more important, to learn about himself or herself. But even so, maybe William Saroyan was right: ". . . No writer knows," he said, ". . . why he writes; he only likes to imagine that he knows."

The Calling to Write

You can't want to be a writer, you have to be one.

—Paul Theroux

Everyone who does not need to be a writer, who thinks he can do something else, ought to do something else.

—Georges Simenon

How long have you pondered the question of when, where, and how you got the urge to first put pencil to paper or to start hunting and pecking on the keyboard? The desire to express yourself through the written word is in you right now or you would not be reading this book. Have you ever wondered if you are one of the people born with a genetic predisposition to write? Or is your dream of a writing career just the product of environmental influences? Do you ask yourself if there is a devious collaboration of heredity and environment or some other mysterious factor that drives you to select writing as your career choice? You will need to read on to look at the so-called "facts" and be able to draw your own conclusions to what makes you want to write.

Heredity

Longinus, a first century A.D. Greek critic, seems to have credited heredity with the need to write. Could heredity have provided the impetus in the case of Anthony Trollope? Although Trollope, born in 1815, grew up, as the *Encyclopaedia Britannica* put it, "in an atmosphere of decayed gentility, mingled with recurrent financial worry," he might very well have planned his writing career in utero, for his mother, in addition to Anthony and his two brothers, had more than fifty novels in her.

Charles Lamb's father was a scrivener. Mary Shelley's father was the formidable writer and thinker, William Godwin. (We will overlook, for now, the environmental influence of Mary's relationship with Percy Shelley.) The father of Denis Diderot, chief editor of the brilliant French *Encyclopedie*, was a master cutler, which may or may not account for Denis's incisive style. Mere anecdotal evidence, you say? Then let us turn quickly from nature to nurture.

Environment

Parents can often, inadvertently or not, provide an environment conducive to the shaping of writers. Bronson Alcott, Louisa May Alcott's father, may have been perennially poor, but he chose to live across the road from Ralph Waldo Emerson, whom Louisa May visited. And Henry Thoreau's father was a manufacturer of pencils.

Many of the world's finest writers grew up in a threadbare milieu, were parented by indigent fathers and ignorant mothers, and subsequently developed the melancholy or choleric temperament of a Coleridge or Kafka. The forebears of others were depressingly wealthy.

Mutation

We have just presented the case for nature and nurture. However, not to be overlooked is the slim chance that a writer might be a sort of one-shot literary mutant. For example, consider the case of a writer born into a family, all of whom as long as any of them can remember, had grown up to be bricklayers. A tidy analogy could (but won't) be drawn between word laying and bricklaying.

Although the one-shot mutation hypothesis seems the most credible choice, the question of a writer's genesis remains a baffling one.

Symptoms

There are some suggestive symptoms to be observed when a writer's career is in the making. Children who grow up to be writers often show susceptibility to infatuation with words and word patterns at a very early age. I once knew a small child (now a writer) who was so taken with spelling that she used to memorize new words feverishly each day as she skipped happily to school. On one occasion I asked a class of young persons to write a haiku, an unrhymed Japanese poem with an intricate problem of word patterning. The children returned the next day, grubby, wrinkled papers in their hands, pride in their eyes. Two or three (those destined to be poets) could be more nearly described as being in shock.

Addictive reading is another major symptom. Incipient writers usually begin perusing the world's literature at a very early age. Think of John Stuart Mill, who during his first two years must have read everything in the English language that was appropriate to his age, for by the time he was three his father was teaching him Greek, and in his seventh year he began reading Latin.

A third symptom appears when an innocent, healthy minded person becomes victim to infection by a book. Certain books are infectious to susceptible persons. Could you have been one of these? Perhaps your reading was fragmentary, until one day, when you were six, or maybe sixty, you read a very admirable but subversive book. It might have been Lewis Carroll's *Alice in Wonderland* or Joseph Conrad's *Heart of Darkness*. Whatever it was in your case, you had never been so engrossed. When you put the book down, your mind was reeling with questions: "How did the author go about it? Why did he begin where he began? How did he contrive to make his vision my vision?" Then came the crucial question: "Is it possible that I could learn to write so well?"

Then what? Were you satisfied just to wonder? If so, the attack was acute. It passed. But if from that point on you found yourself obsessing over the structure and stature of each book read, pondering the author's style, probing the syntax, gauging the quality of the ideas, and (even more critical) slavishly aping these facets in scribbling of your own, either you have been scheming to become a writer or you are one.

There's another symptom—chronic scribbling. Robert Louis Stevenson, obviously a chronic scribbler, lived with words. He practiced constantly. To be a writer, one must read, he believed, for writing alone "set[s] no standard of achievement."

Persistent, intense reading and writing are two prerequisites, then, to becoming a professional writer. "I kept always two books in my pocket," Stevenson wrote. "One to read, one to write in. As I walked, my mind was busy fitting what I saw with appropriate words . . ."

Benefits of Higher Education

If you are serious about becoming a writer and you don't have a college education, it would be wise to get one. It is true that neither William Shakespeare nor Ben Jonson were university graduates. Mark Twain didn't have a college degree. Georges Simenon and William Faulkner never finished high school. But we live in a world buried beneath the debris of a media explosion. It has been snowing paper ever since Gutenberg's printing press, beginning with the tiny, intermittent flurries of the fifteenth century, thick with Bibles and prayer books, right on through the mass-produced snowstorms of the nineteenth century to our interminable twentieth-century blizzard. During all that time (and long before, for that matter) some superior writings have been composed by some superior minds. So as writers, we need to read, understand, and appreciate the standards of our predecessors, the better to reflect upon and establish our own. Only shallow writing springs from superficial minds.

> *As in the body, so in writing, hollow and artificial swellings are bad . . .*
>
> —Michel de Montaigne

Some quite intelligent and profitable reading is done in English literature classes at colleges and universities, where students collectively discuss and analyze individual books and writers and learn about their historical and social backgrounds. It is a revelation to study the anatomy of a great novel. It isn't at all like the study of medical anatomy. The purpose of an autopsy, for example, is to find out what went wrong. Conversely, as a result of a skillful literary "dissection," in writing life is created. Studying the book as an organism, we examine its structure, its various systems and parts. We probe to its very heart. And, thereby, we discover its soul. (For every great book has a soul.) And then, excitingly, it comes to life, for this kind of dissection animates and enlivens almost forever such unforgettable characters as Tess, Huck Finn, Emma Bovary, Molly Bloom, Oliver Twist, Lady Chatterly, Raskolnikov, and myriads of fictional characters, some of whom we know and understand better than our closest friends.

The same thing holds true for nonfiction. A desultory reading can be as meaningless as a glance at a passing stranger.

A college education, then, though not indispensable, could be important to a writer's future. If you cannot finance one, there are loans and scholarships to be had. And if you must work during the day, there are evening schools where you can earn a bachelor's degree at your own pace. If possible, choose an institution with a strong creative writing, journalism, or communications department.

If you are already enrolled in a university or college and are considering a major in writing, but want to explore the opportunities further, visit your school's career information center. Director Jim Briggs of the University of California at Berkeley's Career Planning and Placement Center explains how such a center might help in defining career objectives and planning goals.

"Step one," he explained, "will show the student how to determine whether his interest is a valid one."

Step two involves using the resources of the career center library for some in-depth reading. Step three puts the student into direct contact with people working in his or her field of interest.

As the student investigates aspects of, say, journalism, he or she will be reflecting on his or her own fitness for such a career. When the student's career interest is properly focused, Mr. Briggs said, "he will want to discuss how to reach his goal." That will entail selecting a major and coupling academic work with practical experience.

If you are planning to study writing at the university level, get copies of the annual bulletins containing courses of study at the college or university of your choice. Look in the index under "English," "Creative Writing," "Communications," or "Journalism," depending on your interests. For example, here is a sample of courses listed in the *Cornell University Courses of Study, 2004–5*:

English
Literature as Moral
Seminar in Writing Inquiry
Global Women's Literature
Humor in Literature
Postmodern Novel
Contemporary British Drama
Shakespeare and Europe
The Art of Essay

Institutions such as the University of Minnesota and Northwestern University (Evanston, Illinois) also have schools of journalism with extensive programs of study.

Postscript

Before you go on to the next chapter and actually get started on your writing career, you should take an objective look at yourself and ask yourself these hard but important final questions. They will give you some valuable insight.

1. Are you seriously interested in writing and not primarily motivated by the glamour of success (talk shows, possible screen versions of your book) or by the idea of striking it rich with a blockbuster?
2. How long have you been interested in writing? Long enough to have read widely and deeply into the great literature of the world? Long enough to have tested your interest by writing for the high school literary magazine? The college daily newspaper? Is it a seasoned or a sudden interest?

3. Do you believe you have the talent to make an original contribution in the field of writing?
4. As a freelance writer, would you have the self-discipline and stamina to work for long periods of time in total isolation?
5. As a salaried writer, do you think you could sustain your creativity in a professional, dependable manner?
6. Could you tolerate the insecurity of working as a freelancer with no specified income, no regular salary check, and no fringe benefits?
7. Do you consider yourself sufficiently aggressive and determined to take care of the marketing as well as the artistry of your profession?
8. Will your enthusiasm and self-confidence sustain you in the face of criticism and rejection?
9. Could you maintain the quality of your work under the pressure of deadlines sometimes imposed by editors, publishers, or other employers?

Did you answer yes to all nine questions? In that case, welcome to the writer's world, where you will find new paths to be explored, rewards to be reaped, and a culture to be informed and enriched. And I would hope that as you write, you will remember these words of Stephen Vincent Benét: "A writer's theme must, above all, be something he believes in and will defend; something he knows, and knows is worth the labor of writing about."

Suggested Reading

Aaron, Jane E. *The Little, Brown Essential Handbook for Writers.* Longman, 2005.

Aaron, Jane E. *The Little, Brown Compact Handbook*. Longman, 2003.

Bark, Sandra. *The Writer's Workshop in a Box: The Ultimate Tool to Begin Your Writing Life*. Penguin, 2004.

Cameron, Julia. *Right to Write: An Invitation and Initiation into the Writing Life*. Penguin, 2000.

Cleaver, Jerry. *Immediate Fiction: A Complete Writing Course*. St. Martin's Press, 2002.

Hacker, Diana. *Rules for Writers*. Bedford/St. Martin's, 2003.

King, Stephen. *On Writing: A Memoir of the Craft*. Simon & Schuster, 2001.

Lawler, Jennifer. *Dojo Wisdom for Writers: 100 Simple Ways to Become a More Inspired, Successful, and Fearless Writer*. Penguin, 2004.

Lerner, Betsy. *Forest for the Trees: An Editor's Advice to Writers*. Riverhead Trade, 2001.

Lott, Bret. *Before We Get Started: A Practical Memoir of the Writer's Life*. Ballantine Books, 2005.

3

STARTING THE PROCESS

You have to write a million words before you find your voice as a writer.

—Henry Miller

As YOU WRITE more and more, you will probably find that you develop certain preferences and habits. Every writer is unique in the way he or she approaches writing.

Silence or Noise?

Now that you have made the commitment to write, you may be wondering just where you are going to write. Will it be in a pleasant, well-lighted, comfortable, and preferably soundproof room? It does not need to be. John Hawkes said in an interview that he wrote one of his books "on a kind of paradise island in the West Indies." He admitted to writing another book "in the cab of a pickup truck in Montana." James Thurber said that he often wrote in his head

17

as his eyesight faded toward blindness. Six-foot, six-inch Thomas Wolfe even occasionally stood at the refrigerator and used it as his desk. Refrigerators were shorter then, and Wolfe was exceptionally tall! Thomas Mann was so disciplined to keeping his regular writing schedule that he even wrote during rough weather when he was taking an ocean voyage. Edward Mott Woolley, author of *Freelancing for Forty Magazines*, sometimes wrote in a Pullman berth "with my knees for a desk." Sherwood Anderson, being "not much of a desk man," wrote "anywhere and everywhere, usually on cheap yellow tablets . . ." C. S. Forester wrote in "free libraries" because "it was more comfortable there than in a cheerless, fireless room . . . although they are always full of shivering out-of-works . . ."

If you decide to write at home, remember you may have many added interruptions to challenge your ability to concentrate. There may be ringing phones, doorbells, and children who need help finishing their homework or completing school projects. And, of course, you could even have a dog to walk. All these add up to interruptions. However, you must remember that if you are going to get published, you must be persistent in your writing. All in all, if you truly have the desire, you will be able to do your best creative writing under any circumstances, just like all the other authors.

When and How Long?

> . . . *mornings, afternoons, and evenings, and also during the night . . .*
>
> —C. S. Forester

The material for his first novels, Forester said, streamed down his arm and out of his fountain pen "in a torrent of six thousand words a day." He added that the work was "atrociously bad."

Each writer must determine his or her own best writing time. If there is a best time, it should be that time of day or night when your body energy is at its peak, for that is likely to be the time at which your mental energy is high and your mind at its clearest and quickest. Some people reach that peak during daylight hours; others come alive when most of the world is sleeping

How long should you keep writing? Judging by the habits of established writers, the typical time span lies somewhere between three and six or seven hours every day. Still, unless you are under the pressure of a deadline, rather than becoming a clock watcher, it might be preferable to set a reasonable minimum number of words, say five hundred to a thousand per day, no matter how long it may take. This frees you to concentrate on quality of work rather than quantity of time.

Keep in mind that there is more than just writing time to be expended on your business. There is "getting-down-to-work" time, for example. Ernest Hemingway used to spend an exceptional amount of time sharpening pencils. Other writers, upon approaching a typewriter, suddenly remember forgotten duties—walking the dog, watering the vegetable garden, and so on. Some simply cannot unleash their literary powers without one more cup of coffee. This, plain and simple, is procrastination, and since it doesn't count as writing time, shorten it as best you can.

There are also reading time, researching time, and interviewing time to be considered. These activities are less intense and demanding than actual writing time; nonetheless, they are time-consuming.

Write!

Finally, the best way to get started is simply to get started. Sit down. Write or type something, even if it's only, "I'd rather be hang gliding." Write five hundred words right off the top of your mind. Write about your feelings about writing. Write about the curious pigeon eyeballing you from the cornice of a roof across the street. Write about the tree outside your window. Robert Frost did. "But tree, I have seen you taken and tossed / And if you have seen me when I slept, / You have seen me when I was taken and swept / And all but lost." The important word here is *write*, and the answer to when is *write now*.

With What?

> *I cannot write more than three or four lines of longhand without fainting.*
>
> —James Thurber

The computer is an indispensable tool. It's a pity James Thurber didn't have one. Buy, borrow, or rent, but get one. Whether you chop along with two fingers or can harness all ten, you will at some point for various reasons want to do your own keying. With a computer you will also be able to easily make technical and substantive changes right up to the final draft, thus save yourself a lot of time, energy, and money.

Your Personal Library

Every writer should have at his or her disposal certain reference materials. The personal library you will want to accumulate ought to include such bare essentials as the following:

A handbook of literary terms
A good dictionary

Roget's Thesaurus
Strunk and White's *The Elements of Style*
The Chicago Manual of Style
An up-to-date information almanac
A rhyming dictionary
Edith Hamilton's *Mythology*

You might also want to include some books by authors you admire, whose unique styles or descriptive powers stimulate your imagination. A subscription to a writer's craft magazine can offer practical help and marketing information.

What else do you need? Plenty of cheap paper and some three-by-five index cards. The latter are invaluable for research purposes and random jottings.

When it came to pens and penholders, Rudyard Kipling allowed himself to be eccentric. At various times he used a slim octagonal-sided agate penholder with a Waverly nib, a silver penholder with a quill-like curve, and an office-size pewter inkpot. As for you, if you are going to write by hand, determine your preferences in pencils or pens, stock up, and don't go out without one. You never know when the urge to write will strike.

How to Survive

If, like the provident squirrel, you have a "nut" in the form of trust funds, savings, or inheritance money to nibble on during the hungry days, good for you. If not, you will have no alternative but to work part-time or even full-time while you build your writing business. No entrepreneur inaugurates a new business without capital set aside for initial investments and the red-ink period.

Hardships

Alone, alone, all, all alone
Alone on a wide, wide sea!
　　　　　　—from *The Rime of the Ancient Mariner*
　　　　　　　　by Samuel Taylor Coleridge

Isolation—it's inevitable. There are times when writers absolutely must seclude themselves, must be able to tolerate long hours of working alone. Norman Jayo, a film director, producer, teacher, and scriptwriter, had to leave his San Francisco apartment and lock himself in a motel room for a week to work with full concentration on a film script.

You cannot simply launch into a day's writing by sitting down and reading yesterday's last sentence, just as you cannot get out of harbor and go sailing without such essential preparations as raising and trimming the sail(s) and performing the other operations your vessel requires. In writing, to plot the day's course you must have in mind a graphic vision of the beginning, the middle, and the end of the entire trip. All of this requires uninterrupted time. Make sure you plan for it.

Poverty

That albatross called poverty can be a heavy burden. During his days as an indigent beginner, C. S. Forester possessed but one pair of thin-soled shoes that sopped up winter's icy rains and sleets. With his first check he replaced them, and thereafter, whenever the postman brought a new check, he had an impulse to buy another and yet another pair of shoes. At last came financial security, and he exuberated, "I have a bank account, which I have not overdrawn for eight years!"

Rejection

I believe . . . that genius . . . is both much more common than we suppose and much more fragile.

—Joyce Cary

By genius Cary meant creative power, and creative power often goes hand in hand with hypersensitivity. That brings us to rejection in the form of slips and slurs. Don't let your fragility shatter you. Be forewarned, and learn to control your sensitivity to the criticisms of others such as well-meaning friends and family members and impersonal rejection slips. Don't let them discourage you. If you have a talent, you must believe in it and cultivate it, and it will flower. Think of Forester, who suffered the indignity of having his first three "immortal" novels returned via the postman all on the same day, and the added insult of having to remit postage on one of them!

"Writers have their own particular scars, thousands of them," freelance writer E. M. Wooley wrote. He carried the "scar of the familiar editorial farewell, 'Very truly yours, The Editors.'" Their anonymity, he felt, was grossly unfair; they should at least have signed their names.

Writing can be both emotionally and physically taxing. "I love my work with a love that is frenzied and perverted," Flaubert wrote, "as an ascetic loves the hair shirt that scratches his belly." Writing can be tormenting, wearying, tedious, and frustrating. Conversely, there are those moments that psychologist Abraham Maslow called "peak experiences" and that James Joyce described as "epiphanies," when we experience a sudden intuitive grasp of the reality and significance of some object or experience.

Some books write themselves. "I cannot say the book was written," Thomas Wolfe said in *The Story of a Novel*. "It was something that took hold of me and possessed me . . ."

Self-Criticism

One more hazard—self-criticism. Not just fair, justified criticism meant to result in improvement, but debilitating self-criticism. You can never be perfect, and you may never be satisfied with what you write. If he could have done it all over again, William Faulkner told an interviewer, he would have done it better. What is required, he said, is "ninety-nine percent talent . . . ninety-nine percent discipline . . . ninety-nine percent work."

There are other hazards such as illness (yours or that of a member of your family) and family problems such as separations and divorces. And after publication, when you have established a name and are considered fair game, there may be bad press from reviewers and critics. All of these are hazardous factors in any occupation, and they will test the strength of your self-discipline. The point is that even though writing can be overly stressful, it can also be exciting, gratifying, enlightening, and profitable.

Being Creative

Dear old George Meredith the other day threw out an allusion (in something he was telling me) that suggested a small subject— 5,000 words . . .

—Henry James

I have no special gift. I am only passionately curious.

—Albert Einstein

James was always on the lookout for what he called "the precious article," the germ of an idea. To find the "precious article," you have only to look at and listen to the world around you with "passionate curiosity." If you do this, you will find yourself habitually summoning words to describe your perceptions—the particular pathos of a passing face, the slant of trees on a Sierra slope, the feeling of the mysterious emotional bond between a conductor and the symphony orchestra, the sound of rain falling on the waves of Cape Cod Bay. Let all your senses be receptive. Scents and textures are sometimes elusive—the smell of sun-warmed hair, the caress of a snow crystal.

Ideas? You will discover that you have them, perhaps in abundance. It may have been at least partly the prodding of your ideas that propelled you toward a writing career.

Ideas are everywhere all of the time—hidden in crannied walls, written across the sky. When you spot one, jot it down then and there in a little portable idea notebook or on a three-by-five index card, whether it's an idea for a digest filler or for plotting the world's greatest novel. Whatever it is, don't let it elude your memory. Catch it in all its pristine magnificence!

Suppose, for example, you are on a street in downtown San Francisco. You stop to listen to some street musicians, a violinist, a flutist, and a cellist, playing baroque music. You've seen such people before on the streets of Boston, on the campuses of California, playing every kind of music from renaissance to rock. Who are they? Where do they come from? What is their musical background? How much do they earn in this manner? Passers-by who pause to listen must certainly ask themselves such questions, so why not provide the answers in an article profiling selected street musicians?

At this point, you reach for pencil and notebook.

Suggested Reading

Eiben, Therese (Editor). *The Practical Writer: From Inspiration to Publication.* Penguin, 2004.

Hacker, Diana. *Rules for Writers*. Bedford/St. Martin's, 2003.

Kempton, Gloria. *Write Great Fiction: Dialogue: Techniques and Exercises for Crafting Effective Dialogue*. F & W Publications, 2004.

Poynter, Dan. *Self-Publishing Manual: How to Write, Print, and Sell Your Own Book*. Para Publishing, 2003.

Ross, Tom. *The Complete Guide to Self-Publishing: Everything You Need to Know to Write, Publish, Promote, and Sell Your Own Book*. F & W Publications, 2001.

Siegal, Allan M. *New York Times Manual of Style and Usage: The Official Style Guide Used by the Writers and Editors of the World's Most Authoritative Newspaper*. Crown Publishing, 2002.

Whitely, Carol. *Everything Creative Writing Book: All You Need to Know to Write a Novel, Short Story, Screenplay, Poem, or Article*. Adams Media, 2002.

4

FREELANCE WRITING

I'm not happy when I'm writing, but I'm more unhappy when I'm not.

—Fannie Hurst

Do you like being your own boss? Are you self-motivated and decisive? Would you like to write about a variety of subjects? Would you like the freedom to choose when and where and for whom you work? Would you like to make more money when you write? If you answered yes to these questions, then you should consider a career as a freelance writer.

Freelance writers are writers who work independently for themselves and get paid only if their works are purchased. *Webster's New Third International Dictionary* defines a freelance writer as a writer who writes stories or articles for the open market with long-term commitments to no one publisher or periodical. Freelance writers are entrepreneurs, running their own businesses. And, as entrepreneurs, freelance writers must choose their workplaces, provide their working tools, set their schedules, and pay their expenses. Freelance writers write fiction, nonfiction, dramas, poems, reviews, screenplays, and short stories as well as a variety of magazine and newspaper articles. They write to make a living and pay their bills; however, many do support themselves primarily with income derived from other sources.

Write without pay until somebody offers pay. If nobody offers within three years, the candidate may look upon this circumstance with the most implicit confidence as the sign that sawing wood is what he was intended for.

—Mark Twain

Getting Your Business Started

When prolific freelance authors Marge Eberts and Peggy Gisler began collaborating on their writing careers more than twenty years ago, they assumed they would work separately in splendid solitude and pool their efforts. "Then we realized we both pop gum and work barefoot, and we could get the job done faster together," Marge Eberts says.

However, behind this casual approach is their ability to write what major educational publishers want. Eberts and Gisler began their career together when they developed their theses for their educational specialist degrees into a vocabulary program for students from third to eighth grades. The program was purchased by Benific Press, which today is Harcourt Brace Jovanovich. The program was titled "Word Wise."

Their next project was a book for young readers, *Pancakes, Crackers, and Pizza*, published by Children's Press. "The book teaches shapes," Gisler says. "Our hero, Eddie, turns into the shape of everything he eats. We had to compromise with the nutritionists, though. They said we were using way too much fatty food. So we changed donuts to oranges." Their third project, *Effective Speaking*, which is a guide to improved communications, was purchased by World Book, Inc. The prolific freelance authors have gone on to write more than fifty books that are currently in print at your local library or bookstore. Their writing is concentrated in the field of education. The two authors have written textbooks, beginning readers, and study skills books for schoolchildren. They have also written speech books for adults, numerous career books, a college preparation handbook, and several books designed to help parents guide their children through school. Besides writing books, the two authors have a syndicated education column, "Dear Teacher," which appears in newspapers throughout the country.

How do women with husbands, houses, and children arrange their lives to do serious writing at home? "Our theory is that we start at 8:00, when Peggy's kids leave for school, and quit at 3:00 when they get home," Eberts says. That's the winter schedule. Summers they usually work at the Eberts home while a babysitter watches the Gisler children.

When a deadline looms, all schedules are thrown to the winds. A deadline means fourteen-hour days, warmed-up casserole dinners for both families, and plenty of patience and tolerance all around. "We do our work intensely, and we've never missed a deadline," Gisler declares. It helps that they both have well-equipped offices in their homes, extensive libraries of reference books, and word processors.

The Freelance Writer's Life: A Profile

When I read the line I thought to myself I didn't know anyone was allowed to write things like that. If I had known, I would have started writing a long time ago. So I immediately started writing stories.

—Gabriel Garcia Marquez

"You've got to love it," Norman Wilner explained during an interview in his San Francisco home. "It's very precarious, particularly in the beginning."

As a successful freelance writer, instructor, humorist, and businessman, Wilner knows well the meaning of the word *precarious*. Born in the slums of the Bronx in 1919, he attended public schools there and at the age of nine won a fire-prevention essay contest. "I wondered," he said, "where did this writing ability come from?"

During the Depression he worked his way through City College, New York, and graduated with a bachelor's degree in social science.

He was well aware of his talent. "You have this power, but how do you organize it?" Advertising, he thought, might be the answer. "I started at the very bottom, with jobs like cleaning out the men's room. Worked my way up to copywriting."

And further. He became advertising manager of a large department store. He also began operating his own public relations agency. "I was making $30,000," he said. "That was a lot of money in the forties. I could have made ten times as much, had I devoted myself full-time to my business, but no, I had to write. Writing was my true love, and I'd have been a very unhappy man if I hadn't allotted time for my writing."

Norman Wilner is a natural humorist. He has a knack for composing what he called "funny, nutty, crazy, insulting letters. Groucho Marx–type letters." Actually, Groucho Marx read a collection of Wilner's letters and wrote him a fan letter, applauding his sense of humor. He began writing humorous restaurant news. Writing a newspaper column for a small magazine led to interviews and the sale of articles about a number of famous comedians.

Never give up. "I could paper the walls of my living room with rejection slips," Wilner said. "Save rejected articles and stories. Six months or a year later they may be salable. After twenty-three rejections on a humorous article about Mel Brooks, I filed it away for future reference. A year later I sent it out again, and this time *TV News*, which had previously rejected it, liked it and bought it. You see? Never give up."

Esquire published his article on Zero Mostel, whom Wilner described as a "wild, hilarious, delightful guy." That led to another article, this one on Alan King, also published by *Esquire*. "*Esquire*," he said, "gave me an entré to other magazines."

When Wilner's wife once accused him of loving his typewriter more than he loved her, he agreed. "It's true. And furthermore," he told me, "your typewriter is a good substitute for a psychiatrist. It's great therapy—writing—and you save yourself $50 an hour!"

Wilner advises his creative writing students not to write just for money. "For every million-dollar author there'll be a million starving writers out there. . . . I'm not wealthy," he told me, "but just think, with all the books William Faulkner wrote, he averaged only $600 a year from his writing. Just imagine. William Faulkner!"

What other qualifications should a young writer possess? "Guts!" he emphasized. "Persistence. And faith in yourself."

A Day in the Life of One Freelance Writer

"An average day? I wake up at 3:00 A.M. Put on the coffee. Admire my African violets. Sit down, work three or four hours by hand (it's quieter) until my wife wakes up. Then it's fresh coffee with her, and we chat a bit. Talk about our two kids. After that I work three or four more hours. Hard work, really. Just as hard as digging a ditch . . . very intense. I have a bit of lunch at 1:00 p.m., then a little nap. I work every day except Saturdays and Sundays and holidays. But I'm at it all the time.

"Barefoot, taking a shower, making love, I'm always thinking writing. It's a happy obsession . . . like drugs without any ill effects. The years of experience count, too, you know. You're better at sixty-one than you were at forty-one. After the nap? I go on interviews, do research, go for a stroll, think about my work, whatever."

On Moonlighting

"T. S. Eliot was a bank clerk, wrote poetry at night. Louis Auchincloss was a corporation lawyer. Sometimes it's necessary, especially at the beginning, to have a regular job during the week and do your writing mornings, evenings, and weekends."

That way, he said, freelancing isn't so precarious.

Suggested Reading

Bowerman, Peter. *The Well-Fed Writer: Financial Self-Sufficiency as a Freelance Writer in Six Months or Less.* Fanove Publishing, 2000.

Deval, Jacqueline. *Publicize Your Book!: An Insider's Guide to Getting Your Book the Attention It Deserves.* Penguin, 2003.

Formichelli, Linda. *The Renegade Writer: A Totally Unconventional Guide to Freelance Writing Success.* Marion Street Press, 2003.

Harper, Timothy. *ASJA Guide to Freelance Writing.* St. Martin's Press, 2003.

James-Enger, Kelly. *Six-Figure Freelancing.* Random House, 2005.

Lyon, Elizabeth. *Nonfiction Book Proposals Anybody Can Write: How to Get a Contract and Advance Before Writing Your Book.* Perigee Trade, 2002.

Taylor, David. *The Freelance Success Book: Insider Secrets for Selling Every Word You Write.* Peak Writing, 2003.

5

WRITING POETRY

Don't ask a poet to explain himself. He cannot.

—Plato

In writing poetry, all of one's attention is focused on some inner voice.

—Li Young Lee

Poetry is the rhythmical creation of beauty in words.

—Edgar Allan Poe

MARK SHOUP IS an award-winning high-school English and creative writing teacher who has lectured and presented workshops on creative writing around the country. He shares his tips on writing creative poetry. Mark is different from many other teachers because he teaches his students to write poetry the same way he would teach them to write anything. The writer needs to start with an idea. Then the writer needs to play with that idea. It is essential to play with the words. Also when writing poetry, it is important to keep in mind how the poem looks and how the words fit together. Writers should remember that their emphasis in creating effective writing is to create visual images. It is great when a writer does this with poetry and doesn't get bogged down with details. Poetry allows the writer the luxury of omitting them. A poem is a story without details.

> The blast of stale hot air
> Grabbed my breath last Friday morning
> As I struggled to my seat
> In the half-empty senior section
> I hoped for the best
> A receptive audience
> A captivating speaker
> Cool air from open doors
> Instead
> A noisy crowd
> A cardboard presenter
> Hot muggy air
> But I tried to keep hope
> I tried to listen
> I tried to stay cool
> I tried to think this was
> A good use of time
> But it wasn't
> Lethargic juniors stretched out on the floor
> Bored freshman pulled assigned
> Novels from their backpacks
> Seniors tore their
> Little yellow cards into thousands of pieces
> Scowling teachers patrolled the gym perimeter

Keeping a lookout
For sleepers-studiers
And talkers
The man in black eventually
Stopped talking
We jumbled back to our
Classrooms
Why don't we ever learn

—Mark Shoup

The above poem doesn't tell you the name of the speaker or even what the speaker is talking about; however, an effective story is being told to the reader. Writers need to always remember that their real goal is to tell the audience an effective story.

Exercises to Help You Write

Here is the first of six exercises that you need to do, especially if you are serious about writing poetry. First get out of your chair and go find a favorite photograph. You are going to look at the photograph and start playing with words. Mark selected a photo of a runner tying his shoes. He put the picture sideways on his desk to give it a different effect; then, he started working with words. Here's what he wrote:

His Run

planned, ordered, organized
today the 5-mile loop
down Smoky Row Road
As easy as tying his shoe.

His Life

unplanned, nonordered, disorganized
today, like yesterday,
struggling to keep up
As annoying as a straggling shoelace.

As Mark began his writing process, he liked some of his words and decided to change others. He then decided to tie life into the poem and added the second stanza. If you plan to make your living by writing poetry, it is important to remember that great technique is never perfected the first time through.

Effective stories aren't written—they're re-written.

—Mark Shoup

OK! Are you ready for your second exercise? This one is about writing a direct-address poem. Read the following two poems. The first poem, "Eyes to Heaven," was written by Matt Russ, who was one of Mark Shoup's students.

Eyes to Heaven

Grandma, I guess I never knew,
What it was like,
To have a grandmother,
Baking cookies every time I'd visit,
Sending money every birthday,
Someone to talk to.
Now that you're gone, grandma,
I guess I'll never know.
I might just see it in the eyes,

Of my mother,
When my children are born.
But I'm no longer the innocent child,
That I was, Grandma.
I guess I'll never know,
What it must have been like.
I hear it from my siblings,
How they look back on those days.
Yet I cannot remember Grandma.
I miss you.

A second example of a direct-address poem is one that Courtney Brown wrote to her Grandpa Earl:

Grandpa Earl, can you hear me?
What was the war like?
Were you scared?
Did you care?
Do you miss the boys?
Grandpa Earl, can you hear me?
How was life in the fifties?
Were you nameless?
Were you faceless?
Did you love my mother?
I think she loved you very much.
Grandpa Earl, can you hear me?
Why do you fall fast asleep?
Never, ever make a peep?
Was your life dull and boring?
Or too exciting to remember.
Grandpa Earl, can you hear me?

Now that you have finished reading the two direct-address poems above, it is time for you to get started writing your own direct-address poem. Select the person whom you would like to talk to, and then start playing with words.

Exercise three is about writing a found poem. Are you puzzled? Good. To write a found poem you need to find an article, then retell it in poetry form. Remember, that means telling a simple, story without bogging it down with details. Read the sample poem below so you will have a better idea of what a found poem is.

The Killing Fields of Africa

The elephants are running
months of blazing heat
have dried up seasonal ponds
scattered throughout Botswana
Desperate for water
the tracks rush headlong
toward the Chobe River
After slaking their thirst
they begin grazing for food
but there's little to choose from
Thousands of elephants
have pushed clean some of the forests
that once lined the rivers
cutting a 2-mile swath along its banks
Desolate land
strewn with dead acacia trees
then bark pulled off
their branches broken
their trunks uprooted

The elephants will survive this season
but many won't last another year
officials have decided
to save the elephants
by shooting them.

—Mark Shoup

To get started writing a found poem, you will need to get the newspaper or your favorite magazine. Next, turn an article that you found interesting into your first found poem.

The fourth exercise is writing a skinny poem. Now, you ask, what is a skinny poem? It is a poem with a selected number of syllables per line. The sample you see below has one or two syllables per line. You can decide for yourself the number of syllables; you just need to be consistent with each line.

Lines

It turns
twists
dives
leaps
stumbles
hustles
slashes
drives
crashes
graces
dances
hops
paces

skips
all around my page

—Courtney Brown

It's your turn. Decide on the number of syllables you want per line and start playing with words.

The fifth exercise is to take a phrase like "For sale: baby shoes, never used" and create a poem. Do you think it is impossible to write a poem using those six words as the theme? You're wrong! Read the poem that Matthew Russ was able to create using those six words. After you have read his poem, why don't you try writing a poem using the exact same words?

For Sale: Baby Shoes, Never Used

I remember when we first met
under that oak tree behind the college dorm.
I fumbled my words, Ah how shy I was,
but that gleam in your eyes told me, don't be afraid.
We started dating, I hated it when you were gone from me so
        long.
I'd sit in my room and read up on my Shakespeare, a real Don
        Juan.
And then when you came back, we'd sit and talk
over coffee, Stew's cafe down the block.
I never felt alone, you were always there
in my dreams.
Summers passed and in came fall,
winter not long after.
As time went by, we said good-bye
to our childhood.

Time to move on.
But always together, hand in hand.
We moved in together, apartment for sale.
All we could afford.
Uncle Al, the landlord, always knocking on our door.
Miss Sims downstairs don't like the music, kids,
she's old and stingy he always said.
We finally moved into a better place,
hot water, first floor.
I'd come home after work and we'd talk for hours,
nothing in particular.
Laying in bed one night thinking, out loud,
will you marry me?
Mom came to visit.
She insisted on planning everything.
The words echoed all throughout my body, I do.
We finally did it, the happiest day;
Maui, watching the sun dip down into the bay;
candlelight dinner on the beach.
Then came the news, I'm gonna be a dad.
I couldn't believe it.
What am I going to do now?
We would be a family, I cried.
Time passed by.
We moved into a house, down on Remington Lane:
white fence, big backyard,
neighborhood welcoming committee.
We got acquainted, Ned the boat salesman;
Edna the seamstress, both her children grown.
Boy or girl they asked.

We don't know.
Only a few weeks away.
What could I get for my little child?
I stopped into the baby department,
overwhelming.
Everything was so new to me.
Can I help you sir?
Oh, first time? How precious.
I brought home my gift wrapped in a box,
silver bow.
I made dinner that night.
Everything set out special, candles, music,
a real Don Juan.
I glanced at the clock.
I still remember the last thing you said to me
before you left that day.
I love you.
It echoes in my ears.
Drunk they told me.
Why was he out on the road?
What a crazy world we live in.
We would be a family.
Birthday parties, little league,
white fence, big backyard.
It's hard returning to an empty home,
Seeing the box sitting on the tabletop.

The last exercise is to write a repetition poem. To write a repetition poem, you select a phrase and repeat it over and over in your poem. The writer below selected the phrase, "Hey, You! Is there a sign on me?" to use in her repetition poem.

Hey You! Is there a sign on me?

Does it say kick me,
    Bite me,
    Fight me,
    Bleed me?
Hey You! Is there a sign on me?
Am I labeled a geek,
    A jock,
    A prep,
    A freak?
Hey You! Is there a sign on me?
Are you blind,
    Ignorant,
    Angry,
    Scared?
Hey You! Is there a sign on me?
Didn't think so.

—Courtney Brown

These exercises are designed to help you develop your creative abilities and blossom into the poet you wish to become.

Here are some additional poems for you to read before you begin to write:

Everyone Needs a Back-Up Plan

Always have a back-up plan . . .
It's as simple as opening a pop can.
With one flip
Life can change . . .

The best made plans
Life can rearrange.
Think think think
Everything through . . .
Acting on impulse
You never should do.
So keep that glamorous look in your eye
But mentally reflect upon the sky.
As you contemplate your next move
When it comes to planning
You are so very smooth.
Never, never forget what I say
My words are only to add spice to your day.
You are the greatest
Just ask any man . . .
As long as you keep yourself a back-up plan.

—James D. Franklin

Severed Bond

I wonder if you know what you've done.
Throwing it all away,
Something that seemed so indestructible,
Gone—in an instant.
The bond between us—severed.
Unspeakable feelings
Still remain.
Except for wondering wondering your thoughts.
How could something mean so much to me
And so little to you at the same time?
The bond between us—severed.
Now I look back.

Friendship—it was a bond.
What bond?
Severed.

—Kit Werber, student at Indiana University

How to Watch a Movie

Savor it for weeks and feel the anticipation.
Stand in the line of humanity of smoke and gas.
Fumble in your wallet.
Hear the music of the empire.
Tap your foot in the gloop.
Hand the golden ticket over.
Rip.
Move sightless to your throne.
Land your coat and clothes.
Open your mind and eyes.
Watch.

—Courtney Brown

Getting Your Poems Out There

Now that you have read through and sampled the work of other poets in this chapter, you might enjoy sending one of your creations to the following magazines, all of which accept submissions by new writers. Or, you may want to participate in one of the contests that are described below. Good luck! And remember, if you get rejected the first few times, you're in extremely good company! Many fine poets have amassed many rejection letters. The secret is to just keep playing with words until you find the perfect combination to tell your story.

Magazines

There are a number of children's, animal, and general interest magazines that accept poetry. They include the following.

Children's

Humpty Dumpty's Magazine
Children's Better Health Institute
P.O. Box 567
Indianapolis, IN
(317) 634-1100
Fax: (317) 684-8094
Short, simple poems; pays $25 minimum

Hopscotch
The Magazine for Girls
Bluffton News Publishing and Printing Company
P.O. Box 164
Bluffton, OH 45817-0164
(419) 358-4610
Fax: (419) 358-5027
Submit six poems maximum; pays $10 minimum per poem

Faces, The Magazine About People
Cobblestone Publishing Company
30 Grove Street, Suite C
Peterborough, NH 03458
(800) 821-0115
Avant-garde, free verse, haiku, light verse
Length: one hundred words maximum
Pays on individual basis

Cricket
Carus Publishing Company
P.O. Box 300
Peru, IL 61354-0300
(815) 224-6656
Buys twenty to thirty poems per year
Length: fifty lines maximum
Pays up to $3 a line on publication

Ladybug
The Magazine for Young Children
Carus Publishing Company
P.O. Box 300
Peru, IL 61354-0300
(815) 224-6656
Light verse, traditional, humorous
Buys twenty poems per year
Submit maximum five poems
Length: twenty lines maximum length, 850 words maximum
Pays $3 per line; $25 minimum

Turtle Magazine for Preschool Kids
Children's Better Health Institute
P.O. Box 567
Indianapolis, IN 46206-0567
(317) 636-8881
Fax: (317) 684-8094
Action rhymes to foster creative movement in preschoolers; uses short verse on back cover

Animal

Cat Fancy
Fancy Publications, Inc.
P.O. Box 6050
Mission Viejo, CA 92690
(714) 855-8822
Short cat-related poems; submit any number; include SASE

The Equine Image
Reflections of the Equestrian Lifestyle
Heartland Communications
P.O. Box 916
1003 Central Avenue
Ft. Dodge, IA 50501
(800) 247-2000
Fax: (515) 574-2213
Free verse, light verse, traditional; all with an equestrian tie

General Interest

Manoa
A Pacific Journal of International Writing
University of Hawaii Press
1733 Donaghho Road
Honolulu, HI 96822
(808) 956-3070
Fax: (808) 956-3083
No light verse
Buys forty to fifty poems per year
Pays $25

Pig Iron Series
Pig Iron Press
P.O. Box 237
Youngstown, OH 44501-0237
(303) 747-6932
Fax: (303) 747-0599
Avant-garde and free verse
Buys twenty-five to fifty per issue
Submit in batches of five or fewer
Length: open
Pays $5 per published page

Contests

Entering your work in poetry contests is a good way to gain some exposure. Here are some contests for you to consider. Be sure to follow the guidelines for each contest when you submit your poems.

Annual International Poetry Contest
Poets' Study Club of Terre Haute, Indiana
826 South Center Street
Terre Haute, IN 47807
(812) 234-0819
Deadline February 1
Include SASE
Prizes: 1st—$50, 2nd—$35, 3rd—$25

Bernard F. Conners Prize for Poetry
Paris Review
62 White Street
New York, NY 10013
(212) 861-0016
Offered annually to the finest previously unpublished poems of
more than two hundred lines published in the *Paris Review* that year
Include SASE
Prize $1,000

The Little Bitty Poetry Competition
Shadow Poetry
P.O. Box 125
Excelsior Springs, MO 64024
www.shadowpoetry.com
Quarterly awards: 1st—$40, 2nd—$20, 3rd—$10
Submit any number of poems, three to twelve lines in length
Entry fee of $1.50 per poem
Deadlines March 31, June 30, September 30, and December 31

The Walt Whitman Award
The Academy of American Poets
588 Broadway, Suite 604
New York, NY 10012-3210
(212) 274-0343
www.poets.org
Entries are accepted from September 15 through November 15;
entry forms are on the website
Include SASE
Charges $25 fee
Prize $5,000, a residency for one month at the Vermont Studio
Center, publication by Louisiana State University Press

T. S. Eliot Prize for Poetry
Truman State University Press
100 East Normal
Kirksville, MO 63501-4221
(660) 785-7199
Annual award of $2,000
Submit collection of poems from sixty to one hundred pages
$25 for the reading fee
Deadline October 31

Suggested Reading

Burr, David Stanford. *The Poet's Notebook: Inspiration, Techniques, and Advice on Crafts*, vol. 12. Running Press, 2000.

Ciaravino, Helene. *How to Publish Your Poetry: A Complete Guide to Finding the Right Publishers for Your Work*. Square One Writer's Guide, 2000.

Fletcher, Ralph J. *Poetry Matters: Writing a Poem from the Inside Out*. HarperCollins, 2002.

Kooser, Ted. *Poetry Home Repair Manual: Practical Advice for Beginning Poets*. University of Nebraska Press, 2005.

6

WRITING ESSAYS AND ARTICLES

And because I found I had nothing else to write about, I presented myself as a subject.

—Michel de Montaigne

WRITING AN ESSAY or an article for a magazine or newspaper is a great way to gain experience as a freelance writer. Many writers do not start their careers by writing a book or a bestselling novel. They often gain skills and experience by writing articles or essays. An essay printed in a magazine or a newspaper is generally considered an article. *Merriam-Webster's Collegiate Dictionary* defines the word *article* as "a nonfictional prose composition usually forming an independent part of a publication (as a magazine)."

In the Beginning

The article is a descendant of the essay. For Michel de Montaigne, to *essai* meant to attempt, to test, or put to a trial. He did indeed put something to a trial more than four hundred years ago. When he was forty-seven years old, he became the distinguished father of a new literary genre and a whole new division in literature—the essay. His first two books of essays were published in 1580.

"I want to be seen here in my simple, natural, ordinary fashion, without straining or artifice, for it is myself that I portray," he wrote. Montaigne believed that since all men have essentially the same basic human qualities, a deep subjective exploration of his own mind was, in effect, like holding a mirror to all mankind.

Francis Bacon's essays were published a few decades after Montaigne's. Unlike Montaigne's, they were objective, dry, and full of practical advice on social and political matters. For this reason he has been called the father of the formal essay.

The early essay was not closely associated with the news. But the coming of newspapers in the eighteenth century had a fundamental influence on the development and popularity of the essay in both form and content. In Joseph Addison and Richard Steele's *The Spectator* (initiated in 1711 and widely read and discussed in London), one found informality and humor along with criticisms of social foibles and failures. "The general purpose of this paper," Richard Steele wrote, "is to expose the false arts of life, to pull off the disguises of cunning, vanity, and affection, and to recommend general simplicity in our dress, our discourse, and our behavior."

The Spectator avoided both political and religious contention. But in America, colonial newspapers became partisan in both religious and political affairs.

America counts among its many famed and favorite essayists Benjamin Franklin, Ralph Waldo Emerson, Henry David Thoreau, Oliver Wendell Holmes, James Russell Lowell, and Edgar Allan Poe. H. L. Mencken stands out in the early decades of the twentieth century. Among many others were Clarence Day, George Santayana, and James Thurber. The essay/article appears in all the media today. Radio and TV have condensed it into commentaries and "instant essays" such as those attributed to Andy Rooney.

Let's suppose, finally, that you have decided to write about the street musicians who were described at the end of Chapter 3. Before beginning, to be sure no recent article or articles have been published on the subject, you visit a library reference room and search the *Readers' Guide to Periodical Literature* covering the last five years. You find only one article, published in the *New Yorker*, and since your article is to be regional in its subject matter, you decide to go ahead.

Necessities of a Good Article

Now that you're ready to write, there are several important things to address even before you put pencil to paper or fingers to keyboard; the style, length, timeliness, and succinctness of your article all play a part in how successful the piece will be.

Style

Your article must be well written. The style must be fresh, not trite, and vivid, not dull. The word usage should be contemporary but free of jargon, except when you are quoting. Once you have decided where to send your article, study the general style of the periodical you have chosen. The style that appeals to its editorial staff is the style you can assume to be attractive to its readers. Once you grasp the parameters of the general style, remember that the mode—the tone of expression—becomes a matter of your individual style.

Length

In general the length of an article should be commensurate with the dimensions of the idea or subject. If it is slanted toward a particular periodical, however, it should conform to that periodical's prescribed minimum/maximum specifications.

If the article is too long, Mark Twain gave some advice: "One can seldom run his pen through an adjective without improving his manuscript."

Using many words where one word might do reveals that the writer has given up the search for *le mot juste*, the exactly right word. Padding dilutes your meaning, may confuse your reader, and dulls the edge of your style. A good writer will quickly develop the valuable skill of weeding out extraneous verbiage. What might require a paragraph of exposition can sometimes be said in one sentence of dialogue.

Timeliness

Your article should reflect current popular interests—or point to developing ones. Upton Sinclair in *Money Writes* cited an example of untimeliness. His article on Jack London, he said, was returned from a magazine edited by H. L. Mencken because the life of Jack London illustrated "the devastating effects of alcohol upon genius." What made the article untimely? At the time it was submitted, during Prohibition, the magazine was "committed to the policy of the 'return of the American saloon.'"

Succinctness

Your article must keep to the subject. However interesting they may be to the writer, digressions lose readers. Perhaps your digressions may be appropriate for another article. If so, cut and file them for future use.

Finally the work is completed. You've done your research (mostly live research, too, from primary sources—the best kind). You've interviewed a dozen or more groups of street musicians; sorted out the groups or individuals that seemed most interesting in terms of colorfulness, educational background, artistry, motivation, and lifestyle; and photographed and presented them in what you believe to be a lively and attractive style.

Some Final Considerations

Now that your article is complete, consider the following. If your article includes these points, you will connect better with your reader and find that selling your article is much easier.

1. Is your topic easily identified?
2. Theme plays a major part in determining if your article will be published. Theme is aimed at what readers perceive they need. Does your article have a theme?
3. Does your title deliver the goods to the reader?
4. What viewpoint are you using: narrator or persona?
5. Is your viewpoint properly aligned with voice through a narrator or a persona?
6. Is the action occurring right before the reader's eyes?
7. What kind of ending are you using: open or closed?

The Literary Market

Now you must find the right publisher for your article. But where? Anthony Trollope gave his first manuscript to his mother. She got him a publisher and half the profits. But it doesn't usually work to rely on your mother. His mother was an exception; she was one of the popular novelists of her day.

So where do you begin your marketing project? According to two New York editors in their book *How to Get Happily Published*, 90 percent of all manuscripts are turned down by commercial houses. To get published you must "crank out Top Forty material." So profit definitely crowds out quality. To survive, full-time writers today must write to sell. Writers must understand the vagaries of the market; they must also realize that with a few exceptions, publishers do not lead, but follow, popular tastes.

Add to all this the conglomerization of the publishing industry, with a few large corporations controlling a great deal of the books published in the United States. Consolidation is the biggest recent happening in the book business. Also, big publishers have been gobbling up smaller publishers, and newspapers and magazines such as the *Washington Post* and *Time* have done some swallowing, too.

Celeste West and Valerie Wheat, the authors of *The Passionate Perils of Publishing*, call this trend "conglomeritis" and "a dread disease of the land," but add that the independent, "alternative press" is "still alive, well, and doing better than ever." There are organizations working to help small publishers, self-publishers, and authors thrive. The Small Publishers Association of North America (SPAN) provides helpful hints to small publishers and can be found online at www.spannet.org. Let's hope H. L. Mencken was right when he said, "Literature thrives best in an atmosphere of hearty strife." Perhaps, though, Mencken would have found the present strife more disheartening than hearty.

Think carefully about how this situation is going to affect you, an up-and-coming freelance writer who wants to break into the magazine market.

Suggested Reading

Bykofsky, Sheree. *Complete Idiot's Guide to Publishing Magazine Articles.* Alpha, 2000.

Fielding, Peggy Moss. *Complete Guide to Writing and Selling Magazine Articles.* Booklocker.com, 2001.

Jacob, Dianne. *Will Write for Food: The Complete Guide to Writing Restaurant Reviews, Cookbooks, Recipes, Stories, and More.* Avalon Publishing, 2005.

Ruberg, Michelle (Editor). *Writer's Digest Handbook of Magazine Article Writing.* F & W Publications, 2004.

Whitely, Carol. *Everything Creative Writing Book: All You Need to Know to Write a Novel, Short Story, Screenplay, Poem, or Article.* Adams Media, 2002.

Wray, Cheryl Sloan. *Writing for Magazines: A Beginner's Guide.* McGraw-Hill, 2004.

7

WRITING BOOK REVIEWS AND INTERVIEWS

When something can be read without effort, great effort has gone into its writing.

—Enrique Jardiel Poncela

Do you think that book reviewing is something you would like to try? See if you have the necessary skills to be a good book reviewer. Answer the following yes or no questions.

1. Do you enjoy reading?
2. Do you enjoy writing?
3. Do you enjoy researching?
4. Are you able to compare written materials?
5. Can you decipher what an author is saying?
6. Are you able to figure out why a book makes you feel the way you do?

7. Can you write objectively?
8. Can you condense your thoughts?
9. Can you distill a book so that other people can judge your reactions and determine if they want to read the book?

The more questions you answered yes to, the more suited you are to try your luck at being a book reviewer.

Imagine getting a free copy of a book and also getting paid to read it. That's what happens if you are a book reviewer. Because the job is so appealing, there are a great number of book reviewers. Unfortunately, only a few of them are able to make their living at this job. Counting all the hours of research book reviewers have to do before writing their review, they really only work for peanuts. And most could make more money working in a fast-food restaurant. For that reason, freelancers usually write book reviews.

Book reviewers are normally paid for each review. How much you would receive for a review depends on the size of the newspaper or magazine you are writing for, on the length and complexity of the review, and occasionally on your reputation as a reviewer. You could receive nothing except, perhaps, a new book or as much as $550. By selling the same review to different markets in geographically separated areas or in shorter or longer versions, it is possible to increase your income. This way you might be able to make as much as $1,000 for a single review.

What to Do If You Want to Try Book Reviewing

Look through the latest copy of *Publishers Weekly*, *Library Journal*, and *Booklist* to select the right book for you to review. Also, the *Forecast* has condensed reviews of books. The books in this publication are arranged in categories. You must—always—review a book whose subject you are familiar with. Without that knowledge of the material, no one will believe your evaluation of the book. Talk to the book editors of your local paper and other small papers or magazines, and tell them the expertise you could bring to the review. Another approach is just to review a current book.

The review should be around 750 words, doubled-spaced. If you select the latter approach, remember to write a letter that gives your credentials to the editor. You might not get selected for this book, but the editor might ask you to review another book. You will need to read the book several times and also some other material written by the same author to help strengthen your critical evaluation of the book. Before you begin to read the book, remember your purpose for doing so. Your goal is to explain the book clearly to readers of the review and help them decide whether to read it. As a writer yourself, you know the difficulties in writing a book, so in your evaluation, you must not hedge in expressing your honest opinion. Bad books should get bad reviews. Remember, it is your uniqueness that you bring to the review. And sometimes book reviewing can help your career by leading to articles and even bigger writing assignments.

To become a book reviewer, you will need to be an avid reader. You also need to have writing ability. You can learn how to be an expert book reviewer by studying book reviews that others have written and by taking courses. Just working in the publishing industry also will give you some of the experience you need.

Reading a book is the easiest part of being a book reviewer. The hardest is finding someone who wants you to write a review. Dave Wood, the book editor of the *Minneapolis Star Tribune*, has the names of 250 book reviewers in his file. During a typical year, fewer than half of these reviewers will actually write reviews for the newspaper. And only fifty to sixty will be used frequently to write reviews.

The road to being one of the lucky people chosen to write a review is a rough one. What you have to do is send a résumé and samples of your work to newspapers and magazines. This frequently accomplishes nothing more than getting your name in a Rolodex file. You also can send unsolicited reviews. If an editor is looking for the book you reviewed, you may be on your way to becoming paid for reviewing books.

Book reviewers with some experience, even if it is for just a small newspaper or magazine, can join the National Book Critics Circle. Members' names, along with their specialties, are put into a directory that book editors use to find reviewers. The organization also has a newsletter as well as regional and national seminars that provide information helpful to book reviewers. You are eligible to join the National Book Critics Circle if you write a minimum of three book reviews a year and pay a fee.

For information contact:

Membership Vice President
National Book Critics Circle
360 Park Avenue South
New York, NY 10010
www.bookcritics.org

Reviewing Books for Magazines

One of the first publications in which books are reviewed is *Publishers Weekly*. Valiska Gregory reviews four to six children's books each month for this magazine. At times, the books are so new that she is reading from color proofs that are not even bound together.

When she reviews a children's book, Valiska tries to assess the author's purpose from the text and illustrations. She always reads a book more than once. She doesn't follow any particular format in writing her reviews, but she does try to give an indication of what the book is about as well as an assessment of the book's literary and artistic merit. She often compares a book to similar ones.

Valiska, who is an author and a poet as well as a freelance book reviewer, obtained her job through personal contacts. While attending a publishing course, she met a woman who became an editor of the magazine that uses her reviews.

Reviewing Books for Newspapers

Working in the library at a newspaper gave Betsy Caulfield the opportunity to meet the book editor and led to her becoming a freelance book reviewer. Being a dedicated bookworm, Betsy always read book reviews. She got the idea of becoming a reviewer because she frequently disagreed with reviewers of books she had read and wanted to share her opinion with others. She now reviews about one book each month after reading the entire book to get its essence.

Writing Reviews and Interviews

> *Truly major critics have an influence that transcends the power of any periodical in which their writing appears.*
> —Richard Kostelanetz

There is certainly no shortage of books, nor even of books that merit reviewing. Billions of dollars worth of books are sold each year. But not all books, and certainly not all meritorious books, are reviewed. Much depends upon promotion by the publishers.

Book reviews come in two general categories: the journalistic or short review, and the essay review. The scope of the short review is limited to a description of the book's contents in a few short paragraphs along with the reviewer's reaction to and opinion of its value. You will find examples of the short review in newspapers, Sunday supplements, and newsmagazines.

The essay review is longer, more detailed, and more comprehensive and is found in publications such as the *New York Review of Books*, the *New York Times Book Review*, and the *Times Literary Supplement*.

There are some five specialties of reviewing among professional critics: book critics, art critics, drama critics, movie critics, and music critics.

A critic is an established reviewer who has distinguished herself or himself to such an extent that personality, judgment, and understanding alone will attract and keep an audience. The sharp, original, and controversial opinions of certain critics create a magnetic appeal for their followers. H. L. Mencken, to whom no subject was sacred, was one of these. Commenting on Warren Harding's inauguration address, he wrote: "It was so bad that a kind of grandeur crept into it."

A germane sentence appears in John Drewry's book, *Writing Book Reviews*: ". . . the more one brings to the task of reading and reviewing by way of personal erudition, understanding, and discrimination, the better job he can do." Drewry is talking about cultural background, about a good formal education, about a long and broad acquaintanceship with books, and about familiarity with the various media—daily newspapers, Sunday supplements, weekly and monthly magazines, radio and television programs—sources in which books are reviewed and their authors are interviewed and/or discussed.

Your First Review

If you have a strong literary background, perhaps with one or more degrees in literature or creative writing, you might try your hand at book reviewing. Metropolitan newspapers usually have reviewers and critics on their staffs, but if your local paper publishes book reviews, you might get in touch with its editor. If interested, he or she may want to see samples of your work, and if they are approved, you may be asked to review a book. At this level you will make little if any money at first, but if you polish your skill, in time you can become a skilled reviewer and perhaps some day a full-fledged critic.

Suppose you have decided to initiate your reviewing career with an appraisal of a novel. Before you begin, jot down some reminders to yourself, some steps to guide you toward a successful review.

- Give the book a thorough, thoughtful reading.
- As you read, look for its theme, purpose, and central idea.
- Get a sense of the author's style.
- Note how the book is organized.
- Be aware of both its virtues and its faults.
- Indicate passages suitable for quotation in support of various facets or aspects of the book.
- Keep an open, prejudice-free mind.
- Ask yourself this question: Within the scope of his or her intended purpose as you understand it, has the author failed or succeeded?

Besides fiction (which has shrunk alarmingly in published volume) there are many kinds of nonfiction books to be reviewed, such as histories, biographies, how-to books, children's books, books on economics and politics, travel books, books of poetry, and anthologies. Book reviewing is a craft and a responsibility demanding serious, conscientious work, and there are rewards. As a reviewer you will develop new literary insights that may enhance your own writing. In *Coda: Poets and Writers Newsletter*, poet Robert Creeley has said, "I write criticism to clarify my own thinking, not as a defense of my ideas, simply."

Drama and Film Reviews

Big metropolitan newspapers usually have a salaried staff of arts and entertainment writers. Vincent Canby of the *New York Times* is one of these writers. A first-string critic, Canby generally decides which films will be reviewed. Not all films can be reviewed. In an interview in *Cineaste*, Canby explained, "The space in the *Times* is very dear." His kind of criticism is ". . . one man's response to a work, and that response is on several levels—it's analytic, it's expository, descriptive, and personal."

Smaller newspapers often rely on freelance drama reviewers who cover all important films, the local theater groups, and out-of-town productions. Try viewing a movie or play from a critical point of view, and then write a review of it. Compare your review with that done by a published reviewer. You may be surprised at the originality of your own critical perceptions.

Interviewing

Ideally, interviewers, like biographers, should have a strong interest in the people they interview. The best state in which to approach a subject is a knowledgeable one. If your subject is a person of uncommon interest, read about him or her. Bone up on his or her background and family history. If you are not clear about such details beforehand, you might get yourself tangled in some embarrassing complications.

The degree of depth in an interview depends on the nature, purpose, and significance of the interview and the interest your subject's name and personality generate.

As a college student at the University of Minnesota, I interviewed several noted people for a literary magazine of which I was one of the creators, editors, and writers. We called it *The Rejection Slip*. In it we shamelessly printed all our own rejected literary gems and those of our friends, and even a faculty opus or two.

When George Gershwin came to town to perform, I made an appointment with him. During the interview, by pure intuition and luck, I asked a few of the right questions. Gershwin was charming. He relaxed on a chaise longue and talked freely about such subjects as his love for Ravel and his preference for beer over champagne. My youthfulness and gross inexperience must have amused him. I was charmed then, but I wince now when I consider what might have transpired had I been as adept at the craft of interviewing as I was at arranging the interview. As a music student I was deeply interested in George Gershwin, and he must have felt it, for I was aware that I was not so much handling the interview as I was being given the gift of one by the kindly and generous master musician. This is not an uncommon experience, and if you are going to do an interview, do your research, let your interest show, and be prepared to ask a question or two that will lead in the direction you want to go. Your subject will often do the rest, especially if you show genuine interest and honest respect and do not offend or threaten with crude or over-aggressive interrogation.

Interviews, of course, can be humdrum or heady. If you are deft, it is possible, in relatively short time, to establish an intimate relationship that would be impossible in any other setting.

Ideally such interviews should be held in a quiet atmosphere and at a leisurely pace, though that is not always possible. Also, the interviewer has a choice of taking notes or taping the talk. Taping allows you to observe the expressions and gestures of the interviewee. And he or she must surely find it more interesting to communicate with a responsive face than to view the top of a head bent over a notebook.

Suggested Reading

For good literary interviews, read the *Paris Review*, which has been interviewing noted authors for several decades; *Conversations with Writers*, edited by Duggan, Fedricci, and White; and *Contemporary Literary Critics*, published by St. Martin's Press.

Some top publications that print reviews are in the following list. They are well worth studying.

American Book Review
Chicago Tribune
Christian Science Monitor
Cineaste
Commentary
Commonweal
Harper's Magazine
The Nation
New Republic
New York Review of Books
New York Times
New Yorker
Partisan Review

Sewanee Review
Virginia Quarterly Review

Literary Market Place provides the names and addresses of the book review editors of many newspapers. You can also get some helpful how-to information from the following books:

Horning, Kathleen T. *From Cover to Cover: Evaluating and Reviewing Children's Books*. HarperCollins, 1997.
Jacob, Dianne. *Will Write for Food: The Complete Guide to Writing Restaurant Reviews, Cookbooks, Recipes, Stories, and More*. Avalon Publishing, 2005.
Titchener, Campbell B. *Reviewing the Arts*. Lawrance Erlbaum Associates, 2005.

8

TECHNICAL AND SCIENCE WRITING

If you steal from one author, it's plagiarism; if you steal from many, it's research.

—Wilson Mizner

TECHNOLOGY IS EVERYWHERE around us. It continues to become more and more sophisticated. Technical writing is a fast-growing industry that is constantly in need of skilled communicators who can help us understand the ever-changing technology. Technical writers are found in nearly every industry and work with all types of media. If you have a knack for making complex ideas easy to understand, then a career as a technical writer might be for you.

Technical Writing

Technical writers make scientific and technical information easily understandable to a nontechnical audience. They prepare operating and maintenance manuals, catalogs, parts lists, assembly instructions, sales promotion materials, and project proposals. They also plan and edit technical reports and oversee preparation of illustrations, photographs, diagrams, and charts.

Many technical writers work for computer software firms or manufacturers of aircraft, chemicals, pharmaceuticals, and computers and other electronic equipment. Technical writers can find employment throughout the country, but the largest concentrations are in the Northeast, Texas, and California.

Technical writing requires a degree in, or some knowledge about, a specialized field—engineering, business, or one of the sciences, for example. In many cases, people with good writing skills can learn specialized knowledge on the job. Some transfer from jobs as technicians, scientists, or engineers. Others begin as research assistants, editorial assistants, or trainees in a technical information department; develop technical communication skills; and then assume writing duties.

Through the year 2012, the outlook for most technical writing jobs is expected to continue to be competitive. Opportunities will be good for technical writers because of the more limited number of writers who can handle technical material.

According to the 2002 Society for Technical Communication's Salary Survey, the median annual salary for entry-level technical writers was $41,000; mid-level technical writers earned an average of $49,900 per year; and senior-level technical writers earned an average of $66,000 per year.

Science Writing

Science shapes and reshapes our culture and touches and alters our lives. Science writing is a significant part of journalism. An informed public is better able to protect and promote its interests if it understands the issues it may be called upon to advocate or oppose. Why do people read science articles and listen to radio and television broadcast news and special programs? Perhaps because they are aware of the potential impact new discoveries may have on their lives; perhaps because they want to be enlightened about every aspect of the universe in which they live; perhaps because science is intriguing and exciting, and although they may not want to study its intricacies and technicalities, they want to know in general what the scientific world is up to and where it is taking us.

Must Science Writers Be Scientists?

Carl Sagan was an astrophysicist. If you have read *The Dragons of Eden*, *Broca's Brain*, *The Cosmic Connection*, or *Cosmos* (which became a television series), you know how skillfully Sagan acted as "a bridge between the thoughts, ideas, and ordering processes of science and those of nonscientific culture," as Peter Farago put it in *Science and the Media*.

Isaac Asimov taught microbiology at Boston University. He wrote more than two hundred books, many of them science fiction, and many on subjects of scientific interest such as the neutrinos, the planets, the human brain, the quasar, and extraterrestrial life. He, too, wrote in language clearly accessible to the lay reader.

There are, of course, many other reputable scientists—Jacob Bronowski, Konrad Lorenz, and Thomas Lewis, for example—who have written excellent scientific material for popular consumption. You don't have to have a Ph.D. to write articles about science, but not just anyone can do it. It would be better if your interest in science and scientific subjects was of long standing and was well bolstered by some solid higher education. If you feel unsure about your qualifications for science writing, arrange for a scientific adviser to review your material and to give you advice on the assignment, if necessary.

The science writer is not a technical writer. Science writers write for lay audiences, while technical writers write for specialized professional people.

What Does a Science Writer Do?

Science writers explain science and scientific matters in language comprehensible and interesting to nonspecialists—to people who want to know and understand what is happening in the scientific world. They bring the reader up-to-date on new research and describe research procedures that have given rise to new scientific developments or achievements. They indicate clearly the theoretical and practical significance of new discoveries such as medical techniques and treatments, drugs, and chemicals.

New probes into outer space; threats to the health and survival of the ecosystem; the struggle for a breakthrough in the problem of AIDS; toxic substances in the air we breathe, the water we drink, and the foods we ingest that threaten the health of the human body; the huge and unresolved problem of radioactive wastes—these are some of the subjects currently confronting the science writer and the public.

The information provided comes from many sources: meetings and conventions of scientific associations, radio and television programs, and articles in daily papers, magazines, brochures, books, and encyclopedias. It is up to the science writer to gather information as it becomes available. He or she must therefore read—deeply, broadly, and constantly—the flow of new material in scientific journals, institutional reports, books, and news releases. The science writer will want to attend press conferences, interview researchers, and attend meetings and annual conventions conducted by medical and other scientific organizations.

Gathering the information is the first step. Once the writer has fully understood and assimilated its meaning and estimated its social and political significance, he or she must translate it into clear, concise, and informal prose, being careful to present both sides where a controversy occurs and always strive to remain objective.

For Whom Do Science Writers Work?

Metropolitan newspapers employ science writers. On newspapers with large staffs, science writers may specialize in a variety of areas such as medicine, the environment, the physical sciences, the social sciences, and technology. They also work for print and broadcast media, for government agencies (the Nuclear Regulatory Commission, the Environmental Protection Agency, the National Institutes of Health, and the Department of Energy, for example), for professional societies (the American Chemical Society, the American Institute of Physics, and others), for organizations such as the American Cancer Society and the American Heart Association, for universities and hospitals, and for large corporations like General Electric, IBM, and many others.

Freelance Science Writers

The National Association of Science Writers reports that about 20 percent of its members are freelance writers. They may suggest stories they would like to write or they may be assigned stories by publications or media outlets. Outside the newspaper and public information fields, freelance writers do most of the science writing for magazines, books, and TV and motion picture scripts.

The Science Writer's Educational Background

A strong background in both liberal arts and science is recommended. Basic courses in all the sciences (physical, biological, and social) are essential. Some journalism helps, especially for someone whose goal is to write for the media.

In a book review by Robert Anderson appearing in the *Columbia Journalism Review*, writer Dorothy Nelkin offers her advice to science writers: "Science writers are brokers, framing social reality for their readers and shaping the public consciousness about science-related events." As shapers of the public consciousness, Nelkin warns, writers should beware of corporate rhetoric that indulges in public relations binges, "strategies of control" exercised by scientists and institutions "to ensure favorable copy and to influence the images of science in the press—for their own advantage and profit."

Suggested Reading

Alred, Gerald J. *The Handbook of Technical Writing*, seventh edition. St. Martin's Press, 2003.

Blake, Gary. *Elements of Technical Writing*. Pearson Education, 2001.

Gerson, Steven M., and Sharon J. Gerson. *Technical Writing: Process and Product*. Prentice Hall, 2002.

Woolever, Kristen R. *Writing for the Technical Professions*. Longman, 2004.

9

Writing for Newspapers and Magazines

The most valuable of all talents is that of never using two words when one will do.

—Thomas Jefferson

THERE ARE MORE than fourteen hundred daily newspapers and sixty-seven hundred weekly newspapers published in the United States. About 80 percent of Americans read at least one newspaper every day. Chances are you have two or three newspaper publishers near you. These newspaper publishers are looking for writers willing to freelance short-term assignments. Maybe this writing opportunity is right for you.

Land of Opportunity

The outlook for writing and editing jobs in the newspaper industry is expected to be very competitive. The best opportunities will be in firms that prepare business and trade publications and in technical writing. Still, the demand is growing for publications. The growth of advertising and public relations agencies should provide new jobs in the magazine industry.

Submitting Articles to Newspapers

Every year thousands of freelance writers submit feature articles to newspapers from coast to coast. According to John P. Hayes, who queried 208 Sunday magazine editors in the United States and Canada, the larger Sunday magazines as well as the syndicated publications buy up to 99 percent of their material from freelancers. At best this is a part-timer's market, for Sunday supplement articles (excluding the syndicated magazine sections distributed with the Sunday newspaper) ordinarily do not earn large sums of money—generally from $5 to $1,000 or more, depending on circulation. But if you aspire to write full-time, the income produced will provide help and encouragement.

Syndicates sell feature articles to newspapers and get from 40 to 60 percent of the proceeds. Rates for syndicated articles vary, depending on the size and circulation of the newspaper or newspapers in which they appear.

Checking the various syndicates listed in *Writer's Market*, you will find that their requirements and needs are quite different. Heritage Features Syndicate, for example (Washington, DC), is 99 percent freelance by writers on contract. It syndicates to more than one hundred newspapers and currently needs one-shot features (its newspaper columns are practically all done by regular columnists).

Fiction Network (San Francisco) is 100 percent freelance and syndicates to newspapers and regional magazines. It needs "all types of fiction (particularly holiday) under 2,000 words . . . specializes in quality literature . . . pays fifty percent commission, syndicates short fiction only," and encourages previously unpublished authors as well.

Hispanic Link News Service (Washington, DC) needs "magazine columns, magazine features, newspaper columns, newspaper features," preferably "600–700 word op/ed or features, geared to a general national audience," that "focus on issues or subjects of particular interest to Hispanic Americans . . ." Most of these syndicates will provide writers' guidelines upon request, if a self-addressed, stamped envelope is provided.

Although freelancers write about 50 percent of Sunday magazine articles, 75 percent of the ideas come from the editors, who then assign articles either to staff members or to freelancers. To get an idea of the kind of articles the various Sunday magazines prefer, read each of them carefully. Examine *Parade, California Living*, or the *Chicago Tribune Sunday Magazine*. Notice the slant. Is it general? Regional? Note the average length of the articles. A very large percent of editors prefer shorter articles from one thousand to two thousand words in length—some even less, Hayes's questionnaire revealed.

Newspapers in the United States

All reporters are writers. This means whatever the type of work there will be challenge, excitement, and the pressure of deadlines to meet as well as long, irregular, and sometimes dangerous hours. Newspapers hire experienced and talented writers to write editorials and columns. These writers generally represent their own or their newspaper's opinion or position in their comments.

The Reporter's Job

Suppose you definitely intend to become a newspaper reporter. Here are the tasks you'll be expected to perform:

1. Collect news, talk to observers, get accurate information about what has happened, where, when, to whom, how, and why.
2. Call the city editor of the paper and report what you have learned.
3. Then, either return to the newsroom and write the story, or if you must cover another story, give the first story by telephone to a rewrite person.
4. And then? Perhaps you must cover a controversial conservation commission meeting, or be at the airport with questions when a visiting dignitary arrives. Or you might be asked to report on a speech to be made by the mayor at a senior citizens' center.

Roger Ebert: Distinguished Newspaper Reporter, Author, and Film Critic

Roger Ebert, nationally recognized and admired by TV viewers, began his career in journalism at Urbana, Illinois, when he "purchased a Hektograph set . . . that allowed me to hand-letter a neighborhood newspaper and then use a tray of gelatin to reproduce several smudged, purple copies of the *Washington Street News*." He produced his own publications during grade school and high school, and then got a job as a part-time sportswriter at the tender age of fifteen; even before he graduated from high school he "graduated" to "the state and city desks of the *News-Gazette* in Urbana, writing obituaries and covering traffic accidents, county fairs, and Rotary Club meetings."

At the University of Illinois, Ebert said, he got invaluable experience working on the *Daily Illini*, "one of the nation's great college papers."

Ebert claims that he became a movie critic "through good luck. I was always a movie fan." At screenings of campus film societies at the University of Illinois, Ebert said, he saw great classics such as *Four Hundred Blows, Oharu, Hiroshima Mon Amour, The Maltese Falcon,* and *Swing Time.*

In 1966 he joined the *Chicago Sun-Times* as a general-assignment feature writer; then, with no experience, he was appointed film critic, replacing a retired predecessor. "I learned on the job," he explained, "as many journalists have done on many beats for many years . . . I learned that it was possible to express a personal style while still observing the discipline of newspaper style."

Ebert considers job prospects for aspiring movie critics to be "not good." Employment opportunities in the field, according to Ebert, are very limited. "My advice? First, become a good, competent reporter . . . Then get a wide background in the arts, so that you'll be qualified for an employer who might want you to review plays and dance and gallery openings as well as movies or television.

"I think of myself primarily as a newspaperman. I never really aimed for a career in television, did not audition for the television program I host, and am still somewhat amazed to find myself on the tube every week. I will say that I think the show benefits mightily from the backgrounds in daily journalism that we bring to it."

Roger Ebert's advice to anyone aspiring to a newspaper career is sensible and sound: "Start at the earliest possible age to write for whatever publication will print your work . . . Aim to work for a local publication where you can actually see your work in print fairly quickly, and where you can work beside more experienced journalists. Don't worry about the pay, the experience is worth much more."

Top Ten Daily Newspapers in the United States

Did you know that apart from the *Wall Street Journal*, which focuses mainly on financial news, *USA Today* remains the United States' only real national daily newspaper?

The following are the top ten daily newspapers in the United States through March 31, 2005. The source is the Audit Bureau of Circulations.

Newspaper	Average Daily Circulation
1. *USA Today*	2,612,946
2. *Wall Street Journal*	2,070,498
3. *New York Times*	1,680,582
4. *Los Angeles Times*	1,253,849
5. *Washington Post*	1,000,565
6. *Chicago Tribune*	953,814
7. *New York Daily News*	835,121
8. *Philadelphia Inquirer*	744,242
9. *Denver Post/Rocky Mountain News*	735,621
10. *Houston Chronicle*	720,711

Newsmagazine Reporting

In newsmagazine reporting, the key word is not *writing*, but *research*. Basically, the newsmagazine reporter gathers data. A staff writer will write the story. The newsmagazine reporter's researching entails gathering facts and data directly from the people who are involved in the story and written or printed materials in files, records, archives, and books, wherever they may happen to be. Interviewing, if not feasible by telephone, may necessitate traveling, sometimes long distances.

Unlike that of the newspaper reporter, the workday of a newsmagazine reporter is not a hectic one. Nonetheless, he or she must be an experienced, skilled individual with solid researching skills to do this job well.

Eric Taub, the West Coast bureau chief for the weekly publication *Cablevision*, is "a reporter, critic, and analyst" who digs, deciphers, and stays on top of the industry and the state of the art, which can change every day. "A good reporter has to be concise. You have to be a tight writer. You also have to read a lot about the industry . . . Surprisingly, there are still a lot of solid opportunities for people who know how to write and who know about cable," Taub says.

Magazine Publishing

Magazine publishers employ editorial assistants, researchers, reporters, copyreaders, writers, and junior and senior editors. A background in newspaper writing is not necessarily desirable or relevant in magazine publishing. There is a qualitative difference: newspaper writing must be objective, factual, and speedily composed to meet deadlines, whereas magazine writing can be subjective, imaginative, colorful, emotional, amusing, cautionary, and individualistic. Usually a magazine story is the collective achievement of several people involved in writing and polishing it.

High school and college students who have worked as yearbook staff members doing layout, writing, copy fitting, photography, editing, and typography have a running start toward a career in the magazine industry.

Because magazines cover the whole spectrum of contemporary areas and issues, a strong, broad, liberal arts education is important for magazine journalists. Courses in economics, literature, science, philosophy, sociology, and political science will provide valuable background.

For information about institutions and associations offering courses relative to employment in magazine publishing, go to the Dow Jones Newspaper Fund website at http://djnewspaperfund .dowjones.com/fund, or write:

Dow Jones Newspaper Fund
P.O. Box 300
Princeton, NJ 08543-0300

For more information, consult the *Literary Market Place* book under "Courses, Conferences, and Contests." Your library probably has a copy.

Suggested Reading

Bykofsky, Sheree. *Complete Idiot's Guide to Publishing Magazine Articles*. Alpha, 2000.

Cappon, Rene J. *Associated Press Guide to Newswriting: The Resource for Professional Journalists*. Associated Press, 2000.

Fedler, Fred. *Reporting for the Media*. Oxford University Press, 2004.

Fielding, Peggy Moss. *Complete Guide to Writing and Selling Magazine Articles*. Booklocker.com, 2001.

Ruberg, Michelle (Editor). *Writer's Digest Handbook of Magazine Article Writing*. F & W Publications, 2004.

Wray, Cheryl Sloan. *Writing for Magazines: A Beginner's Guide*. McGraw-Hill, 2004.

10

WRITING SHORT STORIES

You learn by writing short stories. Keep writing short stories. The money's in the novels, but writing short stories keeps your writing lean and pointed.

—Larry Niven

I have written a great many stories and I still don't know how to go about it except to write it and take my chances.

—John Steinbeck

WRITING A SHORT story is a great way to get your foot in the door of the writing industry. It is an excellent learning tool for anything else you write. Short stories give you the chance to experiment with different narrative styles and develop a variety of characters and situations. However, you will never be offered a high six-figure deal for writing a short story. Short stories don't make it into paperbacks or onto the large screen; therefore, authors are never offered a sizable advance.

Did you realize that for nearly every week since 1925 the *New Yorker* has published a short story? If you are really serious about writing short stories, you should definitely start reading this magazine. And if you are ever lucky enough to get published in the *New Yorker*, your writing career has just been given a boost. In an article in the June 1997 edition of *Writer's Digest*, several of the editors from the *New Yorker* offer tips on what an author can do to write a captivating short story. Roger Angell says, "I think there's a notion out there that young writers should disabuse themselves of, which is that it all depends on who you know. This is terrible. Writers think that other writers are about to meet that natural publisher or editor who's going to make their career for them. It really isn't true. The opposite is true: We don't know where the next writer that we publish for the first time is coming from." And that is great news for anyone reading this book, because you could be the next writer who is published in the *New Yorker*.

Writers need to be willing to take risks and not waste time trying to second-guess what editors want. Be willing to go places other writers have not gone, but go there using your own life experiences. The most effective writers are startling and daring with their words. Angell goes on to say, "If you have a special flavor to your prose, it will come through while you're endeavoring to write clearly. We all write differently, and after a while you do develop a tone and kind of writing that people can recognize. That's almost an unconscious process—it's not something you can try to do—from the beginning. I think most young writers try too hard. Try to write clearly, try to write simply."

He goes on to say, "People tend to go in the direction of a successful writer, I don't think there is anything wrong with this. Fiction is changed by the people who practice it. Thom Jones has changed the direction of fiction to some degree because people have read him and seen what a strong writer he is. It certainly happened with Salinger. I think when Ann Beattie was publishing here in the seventies, she changed a lot of writers through the subject matter of her work, what the tone was." However, to grow, writers must look into their own lives for their story lines. Without this internalizing, writers will never grow. Each writer's uniqueness is his or her literary fingerprint. It is what distinguishes him or her from other writers. Good writers eliminate barriers between themselves and their readers.

Try this activity that Erica Jong gave to a group of people who participated in one of her workshops. Look closely at an object around you, and then write a minute, detailed description of the object you selected. It could be a book, a candle, or even an orange. You should do this activity daily so that you are able to use your words to describe unique objects in great detail. This is what you will be doing throughout your short story for your readers. It will give readers a clear picture of what you want them to see. Angell again points out to writers what is necessary to succeed. He says, "The essential quality for any writer is to be clear. Have you said what you mean? Short, clear sentences and a clear setting of the scene are not just the first ingredients of good writing, but are the essential ingredients of good writing."

There are several magazines that are very helpful for short story writers. *Writers' Journal* is one. Every month the magazine has a "Fiction Writers' Journal." This section contains several short stories by new writers. Reading this section will enable you to compare your work to that of others. The magazine also offers literary services. That means for a small fee the editors will critique your manuscript and your poetry. It offers an editing service and help writing promotional letters, too. For more information, contact the magazine at:

Val-Tech Media
P.O. Box 394
Perham, MN 56573
www.writersjournal.com

Also, an ad in the *Writers' Journal* describes a short-story contest the publication sponsors. First prize is $300, second prize is $100, third prize is $50, and there are also honorable mentions. These contests run frequently. If you are trying to get your short story published, it is a great way to get started. First, you should look through *Writers' Journal* at your local library or purchase a copy at a bookstore. If you think you might already have a story, here are the typical rules of the contest:

- Length must not exceed two thousand words.
- Manuscripts must be typed, double-spaced, on 8½ x 11 paper. Photocopies are acceptable and manuscripts will not be returned.
- Only one copy of each entry is required. The writer's name must not appear on the submission.

Each submission must include:

- A separate cover page with the name of the contest, the title of the manuscript, and the writer's name, address, telephone number, and e-mail address, if available
- A title page with the manuscript title only
- A title keyword and page number at the head of each manuscript page

- No staples
- E-mail address or a number-ten SASE for winner's list
- One or more (up to four) original, previously unpublished stories
- A reading fee (The reading fee is $7.00 per entry and there is a limit of four entries.)

Note that the copyright to manuscripts remains with the author. *Writers' Journal* requires only one-time rights to winning entries.

While you are in the library checking out the *Writers' Journal*, you should also take a look at the book *Movies in the Mind: How to Build a Short Story* by Colleen Rae. The book will give you a first-hand look at an author's creative process and will help you to discover your own creative process. The book will also give you reliable and inspiring tools to help you with your short story writing.

Fiction Writer is another magazine that you should check out. This monthly magazine will definitely provide you with many helpful articles to stimulate your writing. In addition, read *Writer's Digest* and *The Writer* every month.

Necessary Elements

Short story writers need to have a plot to entice the reader, along with characters, a setting, and a point of view. After you have completed your short story, remember to let it sit for a while. Then look it over to see if you remembered to put everything in. The article "Writing the Juvenile Short Story" in *The Writer*, March 1997, includes the following checklist for writers of short stories. This list comes from Gloria D. Miklowitz, author of more than forty books for young people, including *Close to the Edge, Anything to Win, The War Between the Classes* (winner of the Emmy for Best Children's

Special of 1986), *The Day the Senior Class Got Married* (winner of the Humanitas Award), *Secrets Not Meant to Be Kept*, and many others. Three of her books were made into *After School* or *Schoolbreak Specials*, one of which, "Andrea's Story" (based on her novel *Did You Hear What Happened to Andrea?*), won five Emmy's. So, if you are a short story writer, get your story and see if the following criteria apply. If not, think about them when you are revising your story.

1. Does your story have a plot type? Is the purpose achieved through ingenuity, courage, misunderstanding, discovery, reversal, or a special ability?
2. What is the story question—in one sentence?
3. What is your theme, the moral statement you want to make? Is it developed through the story's action?
4. Have you shown the story problem within the first page? Is there action in the first paragraph?
5. Do you have conflict through an antagonist, nature, or the main character's personal flaw?
6. Does the hero solve his or her own problem?
7. Is the story told through one person's point of view?
8. Have you avoided solving problems through coincidence?
9. Does the story build through several scenes to a climax in which the hero seems to have lost the battle? Then, does the solution follow quickly?
10. Have you checked every word, sentence, and paragraph to see if it belongs or can be improved?

A Winner

When you read *Ocean of Words* by Xuefei Jin, you read the words of a short story author who has made it. Xuefei Jin is a creative-writing teacher at Emory University. He is an example to all his eager students who strive to get their writings in print. In March 1997 he was awarded the Ernest Hemingway Foundation/PEN (Poets, Playwrights, Editors, Essayists, and Novelists) Award for First Fiction. His second short story collection was published in the fall of 1997. Xuefei Jin has also published two books of poetry.

The Experts

Beginning short story writers would benefit from reading the masters: Guy de Maupassant for his realism and irony; Anton Chekhov for his deep and compassionate understanding of human nature; O. Henry for his surprising denouements; Edgar Allan Poe for his psychological acumen and skill at building suspense; Hawthorne for his structure, style, and symbolism. Others to be studied include Nicolai Gogol, Henry James, Mark Twain, Rudyard Kipling, James Joyce, Ernest Hemingway, William Faulkner, Sherwood Anderson, Thomas Mann, Franz Kafka, Flannery O'Connor, and Eudora Welty.

The nineteenth century, a time of experimentation with new forms, was the time of the flowering of the short story both in America and in Europe. *Rip Van Winkle* is considered to be the first American short story.

As the short story evolved, two schools of thought emerged. Edgar Allan Poe formulated the principle of the single effect around which the unity of the story was to be built. But in Russia, Ivan Turgenev advanced the theory that revelation of character was the focal point of the story. Some writers were attracted to the idea of the primacy of plotting, others to character illumination, an artificial separation, which is, in effect, negated by their being as inextricably intertwined as the double helix.

The Market

The short story, which is often considered a stepping-stone along the path to writing a novel, is a literary genre in its own right. "We have been told that the novel is dead, and I am sure that someone has said as much for the short story," Frank O'Connor said in *The Lonely Voice*. O'Connor went on to say he thought the announcement "premature."

In his contribution to a symposium organized by the *Kenyon Review* between 1968 and 1970, William Saroyan wrote, ". . . the bottom has dropped out of the short story market." The fault, he said, was with the writers. And if the short story were to make a comeback, it was the writers who would have to make it happen.

That the economic state of the short story had definitely declined seems to have been the consensus of the thirty writers from around the world who participated in the symposium. Most all of them praised the short story as an artistic form but agreed that it was not possible, as it was in the days of O. Henry, to live on one's earnings from short story writing.

Although the paying market for short stories may not be in the best of health, the short story is a long way from expiring. And who is to say that it will not flourish and even become a lucrative literary form once again?

Suggested Reading

Bell, James Scott. *Write Great Fiction: Plot and Structure (Techniques and Exercises for Crafting a Plot That Grips Readers from Start to Finish)*. F & W Publications, 2004.

Bowling, Anne (Editor). *2005 Novel & Short Story Writer's Market*. F & W Publications, 2004.

Burroway, Janet. *Writing Fiction: A Guide to Narrative Craft.*
   Longman, 2002.
Butler, Robert Olen. *From Where You Dream: The Process of*
   Writing Fiction. Grove/Atlantic, 2005.
Lukeman, Noah T. *The Plot Thickens: 8 Ways to Bring Fiction to*
   Life. St. Martin's Press, 2003.
McCutcheon, Marc. *The Writer's Digest Sourcebook for Building*
   Believable Characters. F & W Publications, 2000.
Sorenson, Sharon. *How to Write Short Stories.* ARCO, 2002.
Writer's Digest (Editor). *Writer's Complete Fantasy Reference.*
   F & W Publications, 2000.

11

WRITING NONFICTION BOOKS AND ARTICLES

Nothing gives an author so much pleasure as to find his works respectfully quoted by other learned authors.

—Benjamin Franklin

HOW WELL DO you know your nonfiction for 2004? See if you can rank in order of sales the following fifteen bestselling nonfiction books for 2004, according to the *Publishers Weekly* 2004 bestsellers list (*Publishers Weekly*, March 28, 2005). Do you think you know the number one book that sold 7,340,000 copies? Put a number beside each book. Start with number 1, which is the bestselling nonfiction book for 2004.

The South Beach Diet by Arthur Agatston
He's Just Not That into You by Greg Behrendt & Liz Tuccillo
Unfit for Command by John O'Neill and Jerome R. Corsi

My Life by Bill Clinton

Plan of Attack by Bob Woodward

The Purpose Driven Life by Rick Warren

The South Beach Diet Cookbook by Arthur Agatston

The Proper Care and Feeding of Husbands by Dr. Laura
Schlessinger

Guinness World Records 2005 by Guinness World Records
Ltd.

Family First by Dr. Phil McGraw

Your Best Life Now by Joel Osteen

America (The Book) by Jon Stewart and the Daily Show
writers

Eats, Shoots & Leaves by Lynne Truss

The Family by Kitty Kelly

The Automatic Millionaire by David Bach

How many do you think you got right? Check your answers below.

1. *The Purpose Driven Life* by Rick Warren, 7,340,000
2. *The South Beach Diet* by Arthur Agatston, 3,002,597
3. *My Life* by Bill Clinton, 2,000,000
4. *America (The Book)* by Jon Stewart and the Daily Show
writers, 1,519,027
5. *The South Beach Diet Cookbook* by Arthur Agatston,
1,490,898
6. *Family First* by Dr. Phil McGraw, 1,355,000
7. *He's Just Not That into You* by Greg Behrendt and Liz
Tuccillo, 1,261,055
8. *Eats, Shoots & Leaves* by Lynne Truss, 1,092,128
9. *Your Best Life Now* by Joel Osteen, 974,645

10. *Guinness World Records 2005* by Guinness World Records Ltd., 970,000
11. *Unfit for Command* by John O'Neill and Jerome R. Corsi, 814,015
12. *The Automatic Millionaire* by David Bach, 735,000
13. *The Proper Care and Feeding of Husbands* by Dr. Laura Schlessinger, 724,330
14. *The Family* by Kitty Kelly, 715,000
15. *Plan of Attack* by Bob Woodward, 675,000

Creative Writing

Rita Berman of *The Writer,* in her article entitled "Creative Non-fiction Writing," mentions that editors looking for contributions from freelance writers allow—and even encourage—them to incorporate certain fiction techniques and to use the first person. She goes on to say that "freelance writers need to consider shifting their focus from facts to narrative. Nonfiction writers can personalize their reportage by borrowing methods from fiction. Framing a story, creating atmosphere, and using first-person voice are recommended techniques."

Now, speaking in the neutral voice is looked upon as separating the writer from the reader. Writing from the first-person viewpoint is considered identifying with the reader. If the writer's experiences or comments connect with the reader's life, the reader will be more apt to read the writer's material. Since editors want more than the facts, how you tell the story is where creative writing comes in. This way the article remains nonfiction. Since the contents of the article are based on fact and are not made up, you have more freedom in the actual writing. That calls for embellishing and enhancing, narrating instead of reporting, and dressing up the bare facts by using fiction techniques such as setting of mood, providing description of place, expressing emotion, and often incorporating dialogue or flashbacks.

In the basic structure of a nonfiction article, the introduction must grab the reader's interest, the following section should identify your topic, the body then presents your material, while the closing draws a conclusion or repeats a key point. Remember, your job is to write your article like a storyteller, not as a gatherer of facts. You should filter your facts through your eyes, then provide details so that you add to, but don't change, the information you have gathered. Most of all, as you write, keep your readers in mind so that you can angle the story to their needs.

The Narrative

In an account of a series of events, the narrative may be either contemporary or historical, or perhaps both. And, to illustrate the difficulties of classification, what are we to call Francis Parkman's *The Oregon Trail*? A Harvard University graduate with a love of natural beauty and authentic literary skill, Parkman became one of America's great historians. His journey across the Great Plains, begun in 1846 and recorded in his book *The Oregon Trail*, was an exciting adventure story and a descriptive narrative with some current history blended in.

Suppose you had in mind writing a book about Eugene Debs and his quest for the presidency of the United States. Debs ran for president as the Socialist party candidate (a political party that he led in establishing) in 1900, 1904, 1908, and 1912, and then he ran again in 1920, receiving 920,000 votes while in prison for criticizing government prosecution of persons charged with violating the 1917 Espionage Act. This book could be a historical narrative.

If you went rock climbing in the Himalayas—and lived to write about it, your book would very likely be a descriptive narrative. If you went to interview a guerilla group opposing a South American dictator and were arrested by the dictator's military police and held and tortured for refusing to name names, the story of your experience would be turned into an exciting, harrowing adventure narrative. It might be an exciting adventure and nothing more, or, depending upon the depth of the knowledge, analysis, and writing of the experience, it might have illuminating social or philosophical overtones.

Writing Biography

It isn't imperative that you be a doctor of philosophy in literature (or in anything else) to write a credible and creative biography, but biographical writing requires a great deal of skilled research and reading, interviewing, and perhaps considerable traveling. Your subject may have moved from city to city, or even from country to country, leaving behind important records and intimate friends, colleagues, and business associates. There is a detailed chronology of events in the subject's life to be assembled. And one must remember that a human life is more than just a chronicle of events or successes and failures, and that the whole must transcend the sum of all the parts. Toward that end, the biographer brings to bear imagination, insight, and self-understanding, for if you have no more than a superficial concept of your own character, you cannot yet hope to reach any great depth of mature human understanding as a biographer.

A biography need not be impersonal and heavily data-laden. A keen, subtle insight into human nature will enable the biographer to see through the periphery of dates and data to the heart of the life story, to what he or she conceives to be its central idea, organizing principle, or motivating force. Around this center the writer will build the organic structure of the biography, being scrupulously careful not to compromise faithfulness to truth by distorting facts to conform to his or her idea.

Is there a market for biographical writing? Emphatically yes. Beginning biographers are not apt to have the opportunity to write about very famous living persons. Seasoned professionals usually compose such books.

For a historical biography, check the material in print. A new biography of a historical personage will be welcomed if its approach is fresh and its appeal timely.

Nancy Milford's book *Zelda* seems to have been a labor of love, for Milford spent six years researching and writing this biography, and in the process she interviewed more than one hundred people. She had long been fascinated by the arresting personalities of Scott and Zelda Fitzgerald and began, at age twenty-five, to "gather reminiscences" from the couple's friends and acquaintances. In 1963 she traveled from New York to Baltimore and Washington, "into the Smoky Mountains to Asheville, and then down deeper through the heat and pines of Georgia to Montgomery, Alabama, in search of Zelda." Her search for Zelda took her to London, Paris, and Switzerland.

The books on the biography shelves in a good college or university library will provide direction for anyone considering writing a biography. Some universities will issue you a library card (perhaps for a fee) to use while you are writing your book. The number of reference books on biography will surprise you.

If your subject is a living person, try *Current Biography* and the *Dictionary of International Biography*, *Who's Who in America*, *Who's Who in the Midwest*, or whatever regional *Who's Who* you require.

If your subject is no longer living, there is *Who Was Who in America* and *Notable American Women, 1607–1950*.

There are also reference works based on profession or occupation, such as the *Concise Biographical Dictionary of Singers*, *American Men and Women of Science*, *International Encyclopedia of Film*, and *Who's Who in American Politics*. There are literally hundreds of titles available, but, of course, not all your research can be done in a library, as Nancy Milford's odyssey illustrates.

Biographical writing demands expert researching skills, objectivity, loyalty to the truth, and plenty of time. In choosing his or her subject, the biographer ought to be certain of the ultimate public value of the book and of the worthiness of the purpose in writing it.

Suggested Reading

Lyon, Elizabeth. *Nonfiction Book Proposals Anybody Can Write: How to Get a Contract and Advance Before Writing Your Book.* Perigee Trade, 2002.

Poynter, Dan. *Writing Nonfiction: Turning Thoughts into Books.* Para Publishing, 2004.

Rabiner, Susan. *Thinking Like Your Editor: How to Write Great Serious Nonfiction and Get It Published.* W. W. Norton, 2002.

Rubie, Peter. *Telling the Story: How to Write and Sell Creative Non-Fiction.* HarperCollins, 2003.

Zobel, Louise Purwin. *Travel Writer's Handbook: How to Write and Sell Your Own Travel Experiences.* Surrey Books, 2002.

12

Writing a Novel

A novel is balanced between a few true impressions and the multitude of false ones that make up most of what we call life.
—Saul Bellow

WRITING A NOVEL is probably one of the most challenging writing options. While the challenges may be great, the rewards can be even greater. If you feel you are ready to write a novel, consider that most writers who have written successful novels have written about life that they themselves have experienced.

Gary Paulsen has used many of his intense and incredible experiences as the basis for his extremely popular books. He has used such experiences as confronting a bear in his own garden, fighting off a charging moose, and participating in the Iditarod, the challenging eighteen-day dogsled race across Alaska. The race starts in Anchorage and goes to Nome, covering approximately twelve thousand miles across frozen wilderness. Paulsen finished forty-second out of seventy-three teams and went on to write his novel *Dogsong* (1985), which also was his first Newbery Honor citation.

The Iditarod made Gary Paulsen take a different look at his writing. "I started to focus on writing the same energies and efforts that I had been using with dogs." He did just what he said and wrote other bestselling and award-winning novels for young readers, like *Hatchet* (1987) and *The Winter Room* (1989); these two books as well as *The Voyage of the Frog* (1989) were winners of the Newbery Honor citation.

Stephen King, American novelist, short story writer, and screenwriter and author of *Carrie, The Stand,* and *The Shining,* became attracted to scary stories as a child by listening to his mother read *Dr. Jekyll and Mr. Hyde.* He also went to his first horror movie, *Creature from the Black Lagoon,* at age seven. It is not surprising that his first story was about a town that was terrorized by a dinosaur.

Climbing the ladder to becoming a successful writer is not always easy. King did write several short stories and novels by the time he was a senior at the University of Maine. However, after graduation, he was pumping gas at a local service station and working in a laundry as he looked for a teaching job. He was hired at a local high school to be the English teacher, and his salary was $6,400. King sent the manuscript for *Carrie* to Doubleday & Company in New York and finally received the following telegram: "Congratulations. *Carrie* officially a Doubleday book. Is $2,500 advance OK? The future lies ahead." That was in March 1973, and in May of the same year the paperback rights for *Carrie* were purchased by New American Library for $400,000. This enabled King to fulfill his dream of becoming a full-time author.

Since *Carrie* was published in 1974, King has published more than sixty books, including forty-five novels, eight short story collections, as well as children's books and nonfiction books. He has also written many short stories and screenplays. Much of his work carries the theme of horror. He also weaves elements of fantasy, science fiction, and humor into them. Many of his stories have been adapted for audiocassettes and movies. The public loves his work. Anything that he writes is quickly snatched up, and still nearly one hundred million copies of his work remain in print worldwide. Two to five of his titles have appeared at the same time on the *New York Times* bestseller list. Also many of his novels have broken records for the number of copies printed. He has definitely made it to the top of the ladder as a writer! And his advice for you is, "Don't write your novel with bestseller lists or movie companies or rich paperback houses in mind. Don't, in fact, even write it with publication in mind. Write it for yourself."

Constructing Your Novel

Carol Shields, a well-known novelist who won the Pulitzer prize as well as the National Book Critics Award for her novel *The Stone Diaries*, believed that "a novel is a wild and overflowing thing. Its narrative, even when it is short and straightforward, includes a sort of encyclopedia of fact and notation and the gray spots in between, jumping from idea to idea, leaping continents and centuries and changes of mood." She went on to say that the type of novel she enjoyed reading is "stuffed with people, events, emotional upheavals and plateaus of despair. Its scenes dramatize arrivals, departures, births, marriages, and murder, success and failure—the unsorted debris of existence, in fact, and yet its chaotic offerings are, when I look closely, attached to a finely stretched wire of authorly intention that reaches from the first page to the last."

In an article that Carol wrote for *The Writer* magazine, she discussed "Framing the Structure of a Novel." The article talked about how in the beginning she kept putting off writing a novel because she felt that it was too big for her, since she was scarcely able to write a logical short story. However, after writing her master's thesis, Carol changed her mind and believed it was time to write her novel. In fact, her first novel, *Small Ceremonies*, was based on her master's dissertation about a pioneer writer of the nineteenth century. Carol said that some writers write their novels from complex outlines but, she said, "Writing for me is generated out of writing. I honestly don't know where I'm going. The ideas come as I push forward; some days there are too many swarming possibilities and other days not enough."

Creating the Framework of Your Novel

Carols Shields in her first novel used the framework of nine chapters to correspond with the nine months of the academic year. Her character, Judith Gill, was involved in the academic world and was also created to use up all the material left over from Carol's dissertation. Judith, like Carol, had an interest in history. Carol used the same time-line framework for her second novel, *The Box Garden*. However, this novel had seven long chapters to correspond with one week. Carol said that organization helped her keep control of her material.

After teaching literature for several years, just like a builder looks for new blueprints to construct the frameworks of buildings, Carol also opened her mind to new ways of organizing fiction. She said, "I think traditional structures have lost their relevance. The old conflict-solution setup feels too easy for me, too manipulative, and too often leading to what seems no more than a photo opportunity for people in crisis." No longer should the novel be a boxed kit. No longer was she interested in the problem-solution story she had grown up with. These solutions were not part of the lives of people she knew. She felt that novels had to deal more with the texture of daily life and the spirit of the community. Carol looked to create the framework for much more realistic fiction. She said, "I use my structure as narrative bones, and partially to replace plot, which I more and more distrust . . ." As a writer, Carol believed we are living in interesting times and that the strands of reality that enter the newest of our novels are looser, more random and discursive. Writers need to look inside their own heads to be able to build the framework for their own unique novels of the future.

Connection Between Reading and Writing

Most famous novelists have realized the link between reading and writing. When you read, you are reading someone else's writing. Gary Paulsen said he did not start reading until his teens. One cold day he decided to go inside the library to warm up; the librarian handed him a library card and a book to take home. "When she handed me the card, she handed me the world. I can't even describe how liberating it was." He read everything he could get his hands on: westerns, science fiction, and even the classics. Gary Paulsen believes that books had a great influence on his life. "It was as though I had been dying of thirst and the librarian handed me a five-gallon bucket of water—I drank and drank."

Gary Paulsen's views are shared by most successful writers. So, if you are serious about being a writer, you need to make sure you are also a reader. Take the time now to look over the list of books that follow. They are all books that have sold many, many thousands of copies over the years in hardback and paperback worldwide. See how many of them you have already read. Have you read at least 50 percent of them? If not, stop by your local library or bookstore and get started reading so that you are able to improve your writing.

Author	*Title*
Richard Bach	*Jonathan Livingston Seagull*
William Blatty	*The Exorcist*
Peter Benchley	*Jaws*
Erskine Caldwell	*God's Little Acre*
Harper Lee	*To Kill a Mockingbird*
Colleen McCullough	*The Thorn Birds*
Grace Metalious	*Peyton Place*
Margaret Mitchell	*Gone with the Wind*
George Orwell	*Animal Farm*
Mario Puzo	*The Godfather*
J. D. Salinger	*The Catcher in the Rye*
Erich Segal	*Love Story*
Jacqueline Susann	*Valley of the Dolls*
J. R. R. Tolkien	*The Hobbit*

As part of her job, Daisy Maryles, executive editor of *Publishers Weekly*, writes a weekly column that features bestsellers. She says that it is important for a writer to write the best possible novel. She goes on to say that to do this, as a writer, it is important for you to write what you believe in, care about, and are interested in, just like Elaine DePrince, who was not a journalist and had not won any Pulitzer prize but felt that she had a story to tell in her first novel

Cry Bloody Murder (Random House, 1997). The book is about her son, Cubby, who developed HIV from contaminated blood products. Elaine DePrince was determined to tell this story, and she started her research with the people she had met during her son's illness.

Publishers Weekly (March 28, 2005) listed the top fifteen bestselling novels in 2004. How many of them have you read? (Publisher, date of publication, and copies sold follow title and author in parentheses.)

1. *The Da Vinci Code*, Dan Brown (Doubleday, 3/03, 4,290,000)
2. *The Five People You Meet in Heaven*, Mitch Albom (Hyperion, 9/03, 3,287,722)
3. *The Last Juror*, John Grisham (Doubleday, 2/04, 2,290,000)
4. *Glorious Appearing*, Tim LaHaye and Jerry B. Jenkins (Tyndale, 3/04, 1,600,318)
5. *Angels & Demons*, Dan Brown (Atria, 5/00, 1,285,000)
6. *State of Fear*, Michael Crichton (HarperCollins, 12/04, 1,249,277)
7. *London Bridges*, James Patterson (Little, Brown, 11/04, 1,064,378)
8. *Trace*, Patricia Cornwell (Putnam, 9/04, 1,033,573)
9. *The Rule of Four*, Ian Caldwell and Dustin Thomason (Dial, 5/04, 945,000)
10. *The Da Vinci Code: Special Illustrated Collector's Edition*, Dan Brown (Doubleday, 11/04, 905,000)
11. *I Am Charlotte Simmons*, Tom Wolfe (Farrar, Straus & Giroux, 11/04, 775,829)
12. *Night Fall*, Nelson DeMille (Warner, 11/04, 748,775)

13. *A Salty Piece of Land*, Jimmy Buffet (Little, Brown, 11/04, 698,675)
14. *Ten Big Ones*, Janet Evanovich (St. Martin's Press, 6/04, 688,978)
15. *Black Wind*, Clive Cussler and Dirk Cussler (Putnam, 11/04, 653,381)

Suggested Reading

Atchity, Kenneth, et al. *How to Publish Your Novel: A Complete Guide to Making the Right Publisher Say Yes.* Square One Writer's Guide, 2005

Bell, James Scott. *Write Great Fiction: Plot and Structure: Techniques and Exercises for Crafting Plot That Grips Readers from Start to Finish.* F & W Publications, 2004.

Bowling, Anne (Editor). *2005 Novel & Short Story Writer's Market.* F & W Publications, 2004.

Butler, Robert Olen. *From Where You Dream: The Process of Writing Fiction.* Grove/Atlantic, 2005.

Leder, Meg, and Jack Heffron. *The Complete Handbook of Novel Writing.* F & W Publications, 2002.

Lukeman, Noah T. *The Plot Thickens: 8 Ways to Bring Fiction to Life.* St. Martin's Press, 2003.

Maass, Donald. *Writing the Breakout Novel.* F & W Publications, 2002.

McCutcheon, Marc. *The Writer's Digest Sourcebook for Building Believable Characters.* F & W Publications, 2000.

Monteleone, Tom. *The Complete Idiot's Guide to Writing a Novel.* Alpha, 2004.

13

WRITING IN BROADCASTING AND ADVERTISING

A professional writer is an amateur who didn't quit.
—Richard Bach

THE BROADCASTING AND advertising industry is extremely fast-paced, dynamic, and continually changing. Careers in these fields can be very exciting, unique, and rewarding. If you are a quick learner and willing to grow and change with the industry, then a career in broadcasting or advertising could be for you.

Climbing the Ladder

DeNece Gilbert knew that she wanted to work for a large television network even before she graduated from college with a communication degree. So, after graduation, she headed straight for Hollywood. She quickly found out that without any experience, she was unable to get her dream job in television. However, she was able to land a job in the publishing division of Motown Records. The job required her to place songs with the appropriate Motown artists.

This was the beginning of DeNece's climb up the ladder to her dream network job. The experience that she gained from working at Motown enabled her to become a secretary at a major network company. After several promotions, she became the assistant to the director of comedy and drama. On this job, DeNece started writing. She had to write one-page synopses of scripts for the directors of many popular television shows. Today, DeNece has finally reached the top of the ladder and is working for a major network in New York City as a story editor.

The Television Picture

The invention of television might be attributed to a long, long list of scientists and technologists from many countries, beginning in 1839 with Alexandre Edmond Becquerel, who discovered the electrochemical effects of light, which culminated in V. K. Zworykin's ionoscope camera tube, patented in 1923, and the invention of the cathode ray tube in 1932.

The broadcasting of television—the electrical transmission of pictures in motion and the simultaneous electrical transmission of the accompanying sounds—began on a regular basis in 1941. Its impact on social, political, and cultural life in the United States has been immense.

Think of it. Television, for better or for worse, has become the principal means by which Americans maintain contact with the daily flow of national life. It has entered our homes and our minds and rearranged our lives and our thoughts. Next to parents, it is probably the most potent cultural influence on our children. It is our chief form of entertainment, and it is beginning to preempt the newspaper as our primary source of news. By means of its world-wide coverage of major world events, it has reduced our concept of the dimensions of our planet. With its coverage of the space exploration of astronauts and unmanned satellites, it has taken us to the outskirts of our solar system. After Pluto—what? Like Galileo and the telescope, it has diminished our sense of our significance in the universal order of things and filled us with awe at the immensity and grandeur of the cosmos.

Boon or Bane?

David Sarnoff, chairman of the Radio Corporation of America at the time of the dedication ceremonies of the RCA Exhibit building at the 1939 World's Fair, said of the new medium, "It is a creative force which we must learn to utilize for the benefit of all mankind."

Critic John J. O'Connor of the *New York Times* remarked in one of his columns that television is "at least 90 percent trash." Most everyone has heard it labeled "a wasteland."

Today the "electronic Cyclops," as Hal Himmelstein calls it in *On the Small Screen*, is an ever-present, pervasive force exercising both positive and negative influences on our everyday lives. Its influence on the lives of young people is amazing: some consider it dangerous and destructive of humanistic values.

The flaws and weaknesses of TV are of a disturbing magnitude. Its programs, its news, the material in its editorials, and its advertisers' commercials comprise, collectively, a complex collage of audiovisual suggestions, an insistent image allegedly expressing the reality of American life. Its messages and values daily reinforce this image of our society. Since most of its programming is paid for by advertisers, the name of the game becomes ratings, the highest profit coming from those programs gaining the largest number of consumers/listeners.

Who controls the quantity and quality of network broadcasting, roughly two-thirds of what we see? Since there are many advertisers, the networks (under the advertising time restrictions imposed by the Federal Communications Commission) control quantity. As for quality, it is said that the public—by what it buys and what it doesn't buy in the marketplace—makes the ultimate choice. But generally speaking, the choice offered the public is limited and uninspiring—trivia, banality, stereotypes, violence, excessive sex, aggrandizement of wealth and the acquisitive drive, and political slanting by exclusion. With notable and memorable exceptions, this is at least a portion of the dreary side of the commercial television picture as we see it now. But television, through its news coverage, its documentaries, its interviews, and its cultural and science programs, has also taken us to corners of the world we could hardly imagine and brought us essential knowledge and inspiring views of great artists.

Writing for TV and Radio

In this controversial, chaotic, and exciting medium, what are the opportunities for writers? As you'll see, there are a number of them.

News Reporter

The TV and radio reporters' jobs parallel that of the newspaper news reporters', but in conformity with the prescribed editorial style and format standards of their particular media. One radical difference is that although both must be prepared to conduct live interviews or describe pertinent details from the site of a news event or mobile broadcast, only the television reporter, of course, with the help of a sound and camera crew, is seen as well as heard. The newspaper reporter remains behind the scenes.

TV and radio news reporters may also transmit data to a newswriter, who will then write the story. And like the newspaper news reporter, they may specialize in one type of reporting, such as sports, political affairs, court trials, or police activities.

Assigned to outlying areas or to a foreign country, the TV news reporter will be designated correspondent or foreign correspondent. As a specialist, he or she may be a consumer affairs reporter, an urban reporter, or a business reporter. Like other reporting jobs, the work varies from dull and tedious to exciting and dangerous.

According to a 2002 survey conducted by the Radio-Television News Directors Association, salaries of radio reporters ranged from $12,000 in the smallest stations to $45,000 in the largest stations. For all stations, the average salary was $22,600. Salaries of television reporters ranged from $17,000 in the smallest stations to $300,000 in the largest ones. For all stations, the average salary was $32,300.

Newswriter

TV and radio newswriters prepare news items for publication or live broadcasts based on information supplied by reporters or wire services. Reviewing and evaluating this material, they must verify its accuracy and check questionable facts and details. Writers also may be required to consult files and other reference sources for supplemental information to add to their stories. Then they must rewrite the stories in conformity with a specified length and style.

When the occasion demands, writers also must be capable of writing under pressure.

Employment of writers and editors is expected to increase as fast as the average for all occupations through the year 2012. In a 2002 Radio-Television News Directors Association survey, writers' salaries ranged from $12,000 to $90,000. The average annual salary for all workers was $32,300.

Continuity Writer

The continuity writer, working under a continuity director, originates and prepares material that the announcer reads. This writer's function is to introduce and connect the various parts of musical, news, and sports programs.

Editorial Writer

Editorialism has become prevalent in TV broadcasting. The editorialist, by researching and taking a stand on local affairs, brings the station and the community closer together. A firm position on local or state social, economic, or cultural problems may elicit strong pro and con responses from listeners. For this reason, the editorialist must base the editorial posture on sound research and accurate data if he or she is to make practical recommendations for change.

The editorial writer may specialize in fields such as international affairs, fiscal matters, or local or national politics.

Commentator

Like the editorialist, the commentator may record or present the commentary live. He or she is responsible for gathering information and developing a subjective perspective through interviews, experience, and sometimes by attendance at functions such as political conventions, news meetings, sports events, and social activities. The commentator formulates his or her analysis and interpretation into a story idea, organizes it into acceptable medium form and style, and writes the commentary. If the commentator analyzes current news items, he or she may be designated news analyst.

Newscaster

Regular daily appearances on TV news programs make the newscaster a familiar and often a very popular personality. Since his or her personality is instrumental in building a wide audience, he or she must be an attractive, personable individual with a pleasing voice who can communicate with clarity and authority. Network newscasters tend to be formal, whereas local newscasters are more personal and chatty, and they often ad lib.

Newscasters either determine the selection of news items to be broadcast or are assigned them by an editorial staff. The newscaster may prepare or assist in preparation of the TV or radio script.

Salaries in broadcasting vary widely. They are higher in television than in radio, higher yet in larger markets than in smaller ones, and even higher in commercial than in public broadcasting.

News Director

This is the top job in news. The news director is in charge of the TV or radio news operation. It is the news director who sets policies and makes decisions on news coverage and presentation, hires and assigns members of the staff, and is the administrative link between the news operation and the station management. Most news directors have been reporters, assignment editors, and/or producers before being promoted. The best educational background is a liberal arts education stressing language skills, history, government, and the social sciences, with journalism as either a major or minor. Depending on the size of the newsroom, the news director usually spends very little time writing and most in administrative duties.

How to Qualify for a Career in Broadcasting

If you are aiming for a career in broadcasting, the Radio-Television News Directors Association offers the following suggestions for getting started:

- Learn grammar, composition, and clear expression.
- Get experience in public speaking or debate.
- Learn to type.
- Do beginning work in news and broadcasting—a school paper, freelance work in news, or announcing or production at a local radio or TV station on or off campus.
- Become well-read and well-informed in a wide variety of areas.
- Visit radio or TV stations in your area. (Make an appointment.)
- Make sure three-fourths of your education is in liberal arts.

Writers in Advertising

Advertising, like broadcasting with which it is closely allied, is regarded by many people as a glamorous industry. Others consider it a parasitic monster that preys on people by inducing them (often subliminally) to buy products they don't need and, in the process, adding to the cost of those products. In any case, advertising is a key force in our economy, which uses every available medium to sell products, services, and institutions to the American consumer.

Advertising has been around a long time. Its first medium was the human voice. In ancient times criers would advertise the sale of slaves, livestock, and so forth. The coming of movable type around 1450 brought the inception of mass media advertising in its wake, but only after the appearance of the newspaper. In 1666 the *London Gazette* announced that advertising the sale of books, medicines, and other things was "not properly the business of a Paper of Intelligence," and that "a Paper of Advertisements will be forthwith printed apart, and recommended to the Publick by another hand." Thus was born the first advertising supplement.

With the rise and burgeoning of industrialism, the advertising business expanded proportionately. The growth of the magazine market and mass transportation created larger and larger audiences. By the end of the nineteenth century, hundreds of millions of dollars were being spent by advertisers.

Almost every kind of business or industry uses advertising to create a demand for its products and services. American advertisers believe the consumer needs to be informed of new and available goods and services, and the American Advertising Federation claims that advertising is simply the cheapest way to provide that information.

Advertising is vitally important in the communications industry, for the profits of many of the media depend principally upon the dollars advertisers spend. Agencies range in size from one person to thousands of people. Some are specialized, and some are what are called full-service advertising agencies.

A lot of interesting and talented people have worked in advertising. Among them, working at the copywriter's job, were Hart

Crane, Sinclair Lewis, Theodore Dreiser, Sherwood Anderson, Cornelia Otis Skinner, Dorothy Parker—and even Bob Newhart.

Besides the agencies, where do people get jobs in advertising? More jobs can be found in the ad departments of manufacturing firms, retail stores, banks, power companies, professional and trade associations, and many other organizations at local, regional, and national levels. Printers, art studios, letter shops, package-design firms, and similar businesses often employ advertising people. Even small business owners are experiencing a growing need for professional advertising. However, the job competition is keen because the glamorous nature of the field attracts many people.

Just what sort of work does the advertising field have to offer the writer?

Advertising Copywriter

A job at the very heart of the industry—composing the advertising message for consumers—is the job of the copywriter. Copy is the verbal portion of an ad, the printed words in a magazine, newspaper, or direct mail ad, or the spoken words in a TV or radio commercial. It is the copywriter's job to motivate large masses of people. The message must influence them to accept an idea or to purchase a product or service, or have faith or confidence in a business or other institution.

The copywriter studies the product and its potential market—special groups of customers such as teenagers, sports lovers, business executives, or homemakers. He or she conceives and develops the text to be used in the ad.

A copywriter may work under an account executive or a copy chief or copy supervisor, who in turn reports to a creative director. He or she may be teamed with an art director and a TV producer.

Applying the English language to stimulate product/service/idea acceptance and sales is the job and the responsibility of a good copywriter.

Copywriters also write publicity releases, promotional or informational booklets, sales-promotion materials, merchandising campaigns, radio and TV commercials, trade journal articles about products and services, and rewrites of existing copy.

Supplementary to their writing, copywriters may be expected to research information or confer with advertisers, and that of course calls for clear, concise, and enthusiastic articulation of an idea or plan. As in most advertising jobs, a college education is essential to the copywriter. Added to that, some practical experience in writing, perhaps for a college or community newspaper, is helpful in developing writing skills.

What should you take with you as you go out to seek your first job?

1. A résumé, including all previous employment and extracurricular and community activities, especially those involving writing, promotion, sales, or research; any special award or commendation you have received; an outline of your educational background along with degrees and honors attained; and a list of references from people familiar with your character and capabilities.
2. A portfolio containing samples of your work, such as editorials, promotional letters, and news columns. The material should be carefully and interestingly arranged.
3. A cheerful attitude, a list of questions concerning the company and the nature and responsibilities of the job, and the desire to represent your assets and abilities with frankness and clarity.

An aspiring advertising copywriter ought to be well aware of the effects of advertising on viewers and readers. Many knowledgeable people believe that advertising can change behavior and alter people's lives. And the determination of how and in what direction such a change should occur is a responsibility the copywriter must share.

Framework for Advertising Ethics

An "Advertising Code of American Business," published by the American Advertising Federation as a framework for advertising ethics, states, among other things, that advertising "shall tell the truth" and "provide substantiation of claims made; avoid violations of good taste and public decency, false or misleading statements, and disparagements of competitors' products and services; and avoid false, misleading, exaggerated or unprovable claims."

Does advertising stay within these guidelines? Not all advertisers do, certainly, and some criticism comes from within the industry itself. A case in point is the controversy over ads that are demeaning and humiliating to women. As the co-owner of a small San Francisco agency said recently, "Certainly women are exploited by advertising. But so are men." He then added, "It's a bad ad if it doesn't sell," a philosophy that seems to clash head-on with the American Advertising Federation's code.

Schools with Programs in Advertising

Websites for organizations such as the American Marketing Association (www.marketingpower.com), American Advertising Federation (www.aaf.org), Chicago Advertising Federation (www.chicago adfed.org), and American Association of Advertising Agencies (www.aaaa.org) offer a wealth of information and links to various educational institutions for individuals interested in a career in advertising.

Jobs

Advertising can decidedly provide a dynamic and exciting environment in which to work. The employment outlook, however, is perhaps not quite as exciting. Although employment in advertising is expected to increase faster than the average for all occupations, most openings will result from replacement of workers who transfer to other occupations or leave the labor force because of retirement or other reasons. To fill these jobs, the highly qualified and experienced applicant will be favored.

Advertising-Related Publications

Advertising Age
711 Third Avenue
New York, NY 10017-4036
www.adage.com

Broadcasting and Cable
P.O. Box 5655
Harlan, IA 51593
www.broadcastingcable.com

Editor and Publisher
770 Broadway
New York, NY 10003
www.editorandpublisher.com

Suggested Reading

Cappon, Rene J. *Associated Press Guide to Newswriting: The Resource for Professional Journalists.* ARCO, 2000.
Fedler, Fred. *Reporting for the Media.* Oxford University Press, 2004.

Gabay, J. Jonathan. *Teach Yourself Copywriting*, third edition. McGraw-Hill, 2003.

Goldberg, Lee. *Successful Television Writing* (Wiley Books for Writers Series). John Wiley & Sons, 2003.

Kant, Garth. *How to Write Television News*. McGraw-Hill, 2005.

White, Ted. *Broadcast News Writing, Reporting, and Producing*, third edition. Focal Press, 2001.

14

SCREENWRITING AND PLAYWRITING

When a play enters my consciousness, it is already a fairly well-developed fetus. I don't put a word down until the play seems ready to be written.

—Edward Albee

EVERY TELEVISION SHOW or movie that you watch begins with a script, which is written by a screenwriter. Screenwriters are the people who research, create, and write the plot and narrative synopsis of what you will be watching. The script is a blueprint for production. The complete script is typed in two columns: "audio" on the right and "video" on the left. The column on the right contains the dialogue or narration, along with the instructions for music and sound effects. The column on the left contains the instructions for visuals, along with information on timing, set descriptions, and directions for the actors. For a script to make sense, both sides must be read. Screenwriters often adapt books and plays for film and television dramatization. Writers in these areas must follow a rigid style and be able to write in a powerful and imaginative way.

Writing scripts can provide lucrative financial rewards; however, competition is fierce in the field. Cable television is opening up new opportunities for screenwriters. The field of educational and training videos along with advertising agencies should not be overlooked as places that can offer would-be screenwriters employment.

Writer's Digest and publications like *The Dramatists Guild Quarterly, Information for Playwrights,* and *Scriptwriter News* contain lists of what different playwrights are interested in finding. Most professional and amateur productions pay the scriptwriter a percentage of the total box office receipts as royalties; 5 to 10 percent are the usual royalty rates. Sometimes a writer will be offered a buyout.

Scripts for the Screens

A screenwriter is a scriptwriter who wants to break into motion pictures. According to the *Dictionary of Occupational Titles,* here's what he or she does:

> Writes scripts for motion pictures or television: Selects subject and theme for script based on personal interest or assignment. Conducts research to obtain accurate factual background information and authentic detail. Writes plot outline, narrative synopsis, or treatment and submits for approval. Confers with PRODUCER (motion pic.) or PRODUCER (radio & tv broad.) and DIRECTOR, MOTION PICTURE (motion pic.) or DIRECTOR, TELEVISION (radio & tv broad.) regarding script development, revisions, and other changes. Writes one or more drafts of script. May work in collaboration with other writers. May adapt books or plays into scripts for use in television or motion picture production. May write continuity or comedy routines. May specialize in particular type of script or writing.

Writing for the Small Screen

Although the freelance television market is difficult to crack, there are ways to break in and snare those lucrative assignments, says Andy Edmonds. She ought to know. She is a writer/producer who has worked on both network and cable television. In her *Writer's Digest* article "Breaking into TV Scriptwriting," Edmonds suggests rules that will help "point you in the right direction." In summary, they are:

- Write a sample script—an episode of a TV series (an established one, not a new one) currently in production.
- Get an agent.
- Be aggressively persistent.
- Be prepared to meet with producers and "pitch" story ideas and to elaborate fully on any ideas you present.

Edmonds elaborates on each point—how to choose the right series for your sample, how to approach the writing of your script, how to get the best agent as a new writer, and what you can earn. In the second part of this article, Bob Ellison writes, "It is among the most coveted of all writing assignments—the go-ahead to create an episode for a network television series. It's one of the most profitable, too . . ."

What About Hollywood?

Ben Stein wrote a somewhat sobering book about Hollywood writers. In it he reveals some interesting facts. The writers of network shows number only a few hundred. One, Stephen Kandel, who was interviewed by Stein, has written pilots and scripts for a number of popular shows. According to Stein, all of the regular working writers have a "unified, idiosyncratic view of life, and almost all of them live in Los Angeles." Their views, Stein writes, "could not possibly be the dreams of a nation." TV, then, mirrors what these few people think.

It was estimated that only eight out of twenty good scripts got to be pilots, and only two became series. Of these, the most durable, according to Stein, were situation comedies and adventure shows. Scripts then and now are almost never the work of one person, and the writer has very little control over the finished product. In *Reel People* by Mark Litwak, one apparently successful screenwriter commented: "They ruin your stories. They massacre your ideas. They prostitute your art. They trample your pride. And what do you get for it? A fortune."

Desire to Become a Screenwriter

With a degree in film, radio, and television in hand, Randy Kornfield entered the job market with the desire to become a screenwriter. A friend got him a part-time job duplicating scripts at a studio. Then he was promoted to the mailroom. During this time, he was meeting people and deciding where he wanted to work, as well as trying to write screenplays. A move to another studio brought Randy a job as a secretary and assistant in personnel. At this job, he met a story editor who let him read some scripts and write coverages. This gave him the chance to see what good and bad scripts were like, as well as what kind of scripts were being bought.

When this job folded, Randy became a freelance story analyst. Then he found a job at another studio as an assistant to an executive who was looking for scripts. At this job, which was primarily secretarial, he was able to read some scripts but didn't have to write coverages. After management changes at the studio, Randy was out of a job again. He next found a job as a story analyst at a nonunion studio. Then he was able to get a story analyst job at MGM, a union studio. The advantage of working at a union studio is better pay plus benefits. Unfortunately, it is very difficult to get in the story analyst union.

During all this time, Randy was busy writing and actually sold a screenplay and had a low-budget movie made from one of his scripts. Reading scripts has been helpful in his writing. Today, Randy is working at 20th Century Fox as a story analyst. He still writes in his spare time. His writing success continues. He has had two more movies produced on television.

Writing Plays

Aristotle, as John Howard Lawson said, is "the Bible of playwriting technique." For centuries, Aristotle's *Poetics* has been pored over, analyzed, and interpreted, perhaps in as many conflicting ways as the Bible itself. The beginning playwright ought to peruse the playwright's bible, and when viewing or reading a play, note the degree to which Aristotle's ideas on structure, style, and action, conceived more than two thousand years ago, are and are not applied today by contemporary playwrights.

Because of religious prejudice against the stage, which was thought to be unedifying and even dissolute, no plays by American playwrights were produced in the colonies until 1766, when *The Prince of Parthia* was staged. None followed until after the American Revolution. Of those written but not produced, some served as pro- and antirebel propaganda. Today there is no problem with the morality of the theater—that is, our society no longer discourages all playwriting as an immoral activity.

The U.S. Department of Labor's *Dictionary of Occupational Titles* provides the following definition of a playwright:

> Writes original plays, such as tragedies, comedies, or dramas, or adapts themes from fictional, historical, or narrative sources, for dramatic presentation: Writes plays, usually involving action, conflict, purpose, and resolution, to depict series of events from imaginary or real life. Writes dialogue and describes action to be followed during enactment of play. Revises script during rehearsals and preparation for initial showing.

Hurdles

Very few playwrights I know make their living solely from the theatre . . .

—Robert Anderson

For the young playwright the obstacles blocking success are formidable, though not impossible. To begin with, the playwright, like other freelancers, must, as Robert Anderson says, be a moonlighter. Writing what you believe to be a good play is only the first step. Next there is the business of finding a producer (a feat that even successful playwrights often fail to perform).

If you clear this hurdle, there are then the many difficulties of play production to address: the huge expense of theater, director, actors, and music. Once all these problems have been resolved comes the first night—and the play's subsequent review. And one bad review from the *New York Times* critic, says Anderson, can "finish off your play."

This is not meant to discourage. There are many opportunities for playwrights today. It is advantageous for the beginner to become involved with a local theater group, meet theater-minded people, and perhaps get his or her play produced. This definitely counts with a publisher. The more you can learn about all the aspects of playwriting and play production, the better for your future.

Community Production Options

If you think your play is ready for production, investigate civic theater groups, community theaters, and college and university drama groups in your area that are seeking plays to produce. You will not be royally paid, but you will have the exciting pleasure of seeing your characters transformed from words to flesh and of observing the dramatic action you had previously only been able to imagine.

Many theaters are seeking new plays. However, before submitting a play, make sure that the theater is still in the market for material. To give you an idea what types of plays theaters are looking for, here are two examples:

Woolly Mammoth Theatre Company
1401 Church Street NW
Washington, DC 20005

"We look for plays that depart from traditional categories in some way . . . Apart from an innovative approach, there is no formula. One-acts are not used. Cast limit of 8; no unusually expensive gimmicks. Pays 5 percent royalty."

The Ensemble Studio Theatre
549 West 52nd Street
New York, NY 10019

"Full lengths and one-acts with strong dramatic actions and situations. Reports in three months. Pays $80 to $1,000."

Publishers

Play publishers put plays into print and thereby make them available (for a price) to anyone anywhere who may want to produce them on stage. This is done on a royalty basis, with the publisher charging the theater a set rate and usually splitting the sum with the author.

Walter H. Baker Company in Boston, for example, wants "scripts for amateur production: one-act plays for competition, children's plays, religious drama, monologues, readings, and recitations."

Samuel French (New York) wants "full-length plays for dinner, community, stock, college, high school, and church theatres. One-act plays (30 to 60 minutes) for high school and college theatres. Children's plays, 45 to 75 minutes. Payment is on a royalty basis."

Suggested Reading

Atchity, Kenneth. *Writing Treatments That Sell: How to Create and Market Your Story Ideas to the Motion Picture and TV Industry.* Henry Holt, 2003.

The Brothers Heimberg. *The Official Movie Plot Generator: 27,000 Hilarious Movie Plot Combinations.* Brothers Heimberg Publishing, 2004.

Gilles, D. B. B. *The Screenwriter Within: How to Turn the Movie in Your Head into a Saleable Screenplay.* Crown Publishing, 2000.

Goldberg, Lee. *Successful Television Writing* (Wiley Books for Writers Series). John Wiley & Sons, 2003.

Russin, Robin U. *Screenplay: Writing the Picture*. Silman-James Press, 2003.

Schellhardt, Laura. *Screenwriting for Dummies*. John Wiley & Sons, 2003.

Seger, Linda. *Advanced Screenwriting: Raising Your Script to the Academy Award Level*. Silman-James Press, 2003.

Whitcomb, Cynthia, and Philip Martin. *Writer's Guide to Writing Your Screenplay: How to Write Great Screenplays for Movies and Television*. Watson-Guptill Publications, 2002.

15

GETTING YOUR
WRITING PUBLISHED

Forget all the rules. Forget about being published. Write for your-self and celebrate writing.

—Melinda Haynes

Nothing stinks like a pile of unpublished writing.

—Sylvia Plath

FREELANCE WRITERS HOPING to be published in today's extremely competitive world of freelance writing must be willing to go the extra mile to size up what a publication is looking for. Each magazine, newspaper, or book company has its own unique slant, point of view, or set of beliefs. Each appeals to a particular reading audience. If you want to be published, you must be willing to write what they want to publish. For example, the editors of *Powerboat Magazine* wouldn't stop the presses for an article on "Canoeing with Marquette and Joliet," or "Whitewater Rafting on Oregon's Roaring River." However, the editors of that publication would definitely be willing to read and consider publishing an article on "New Speedboat Engines."

Getting your first article in print is usually the hardest, and many freelance authors have very little income as they diligently try to get published. If you are struggling right now, don't give up; you might just be writing a bestselling novel like Alex Haley did. Did you know that Alex Haley, the author of *Roots*, at one point in his life had only two cans of sardines and eighteen cents to his name?

Helpful Hints

If you are truly serious about getting your work published, invest in the "freelance bible." That is, go out and purchase the newest edition of *Writer's Market* at your local bookstore. *Writer's Market* comes with a CD-ROM for Windows that will provide you with access to the most comprehensive listings on royalties, advances, and pay rates along with submission guidelines and editorial needs. And, best of all, at your fingertips, you will have all the necessary contact information including addresses, phone numbers, websites, and e-mail addresses of more than eight thousand contacts of places to publish your work. You can also find this book at your local library, but freelance authors often are working long hours after the library has shut its doors. And when you're on a roll, you really want nothing to stand in your way of success.

Writer's Market not only tells you the name of the magazine, but it also gives you the address, phone number, editor's name, how much of the magazine is written by freelancers, the number of times the magazine is published, the audience of the magazine, and even what the magazine pays. Here's an example of what you would find if you leafed through a current *Writer's Market*:

Men's Fitness, Men's Fitness, Inc., 21100 Erwin St., Woodland Hills CA 91356-3712. (818) 884-6800. Fax: (818) 704-5734. Editor-in-Chief: Peter Sikowitz. Editorial Assistant: Bobby Lee. 95% freelance written. Works with small number of new/unpublished writers each year. Monthly magazine for health-conscious men ages 18-45. Provides reliable, entertaining guidance for the active male in all areas of lifestyle. Estab. 1984. Circ. 315,000. Pays 1 month after acceptance. Publishes ms an average of 4 months after acceptance. Offers 33% kill fee. Buys all rights. Submit seasonal material 4 months in advance. Reports in 2 months. Writer's guidelines for 9 x 12 SASE.

Nonfiction: Service, informative, inspirational and scientific studies written for men. Few interviews or regional news unless extraordinary. Query with published clips. Length: 1,200-1,800 words. Pays $500-$1,000.

Columns/Departments: Nutrition, Mind, Appearance, Sexuality, Health, Length: 1,200-1,500 words. Pays $400-500.

Tips: "Be sure to know the magazine before sending in queries."

Writer's Market will let you know how to submit to *The Saturday Evening Post* or to *Forbes*. Read the following list of publications and circle the ten that you think are written 90 percent or more by freelancers:

American Civil War
Byte
Children's Playmate
Cobblestone
Crochet World
Cruising World
Family Circle
Glamour
Golf Digest

Ladies' Home Journal
Mad
McCall's
Popular Mechanics
Readers Review
Redbook
Sail
Scottish Life
Scouting
Seventeen
Shape
Ski Magazine
Smithsonian
Splash Magazine
Sports Illustrated for Kids
The Sun
U.S. Kids
VFW Magazine
The Walking Magazine
Wildlife Art
Working Mothers
The Yoga Journal

Check your answers and see how many you got right.

1. *American Civil War*—95 percent
2. *Cobblestone*—100 percent
3. *Crochet World*—100 percent
4. *Mad*—100 percent
5. *McCall's*—90 percent

6. *Redbook*—90 percent
7. *Scouting*—90 percent
8. *Smithsonian*—90 percent
9. *The Sun*—90 percent
10. *Working Mothers*—90 percent

If you are interested as a freelance writer, the percentage of free-lancers used as writers for the other magazines are:

Byte—50 percent
Children's Playmate—75 percent
Cruising World—70 percent
Family Circle—70 percent
Glamour—75 percent
Golf Digest—30 percent
Ladies' Home Journal—50 percent
Popular Mechanics—10 percent
Readers Review—75 percent
Sail—50 percent
Scottish Life—80 percent
Seventeen—70 percent
Shape—70 percent
Ski Magazine—15 percent
Splash Magazine—20 percent
Sports Illustrated for Kids—20 percent
U.S. Kids—50 percent
VFW—40 percent
The Walking Magazine—60 percent
Wildlife Art—80 percent
The Yoga Journal—75 percent

Also *Reader's Digest*, *Weight Watchers Magazine*, *Boys' Life*, and *Esquire* were four of the magazines ranked as some of the best markets for freelance writers by *The Writer* magazine.

Boundless Research

Freelance authors will find a treasure trove of resources at their fingertips when they get on the World Wide Web. Definitely, if you are a serious freelance author and want to get into the business, you will need to discover the information awaiting you on the Internet. You will be able to receive advice from published authors and even have online chats with agents and editors.

The list is endless; however, if you are new to the Internet, you might want to look at a few of the following websites to get you started. Many of these websites have jump-off points to many other writing-related sites. By using your mouse to point and click, you will be instantly connected to the cited Web page. Check out these sites for more information:

Writers Resource Center
www.writersresourcecenter.com

WritersNet
www.writers.net

Publishers' Catalogues
www.lights.com/publisher

Helpful Publications

Another good source of information for an eager freelance author is to go to a library or bookstore and check out some of the publications. In one recent issue, *Writer's Journal* had articles on "Back Doors into Publishing," "Getting an Agent," "For Beginners Only," and "Surviving as a Freelance Writer—Ten Essential Tips to Keep You Inspired." *Writer's Digest* also had an article on "The Idea Toolbox." This article talks about the tools you already have in your brain that will help you to be more creative. There are other articles on "Getting a Ph.D. in Creativity," "What Am I Doing Right? What Am I Doing Wrong?," and "The Transforming Power of the Rewrite." *The Writer* recently had an article entitled "513 Publishers Are Looking for Your Book," wherein Pulitzer-prize winner Carol Shields discussed how to frame the structure of your novel, how to get a literary agent, and how to make the poet's choice— lyric or narrative. These and many more publications can easily be found at your local library.

Editorial Advice

"Get to know the editor" is the advice from Wendy Strothman, president of Beacon Press. She went on to say that her company "looks for books other houses may be missing. Our books come through writers as often as they come from agents." She went on to advise writers, "Don't let agents do all the negotiating. Get to know the editor who wants to buy your book, and make sure that not only the editor but the house is behind your book, in case the editor leaves."

Mailing Off Your Writing

Do you think that just because you have completed your research, written your article, and know exactly where you are sending it, your job is finished? Wrong! There is more to do before you can sit back and relax. You need to write a special letter to enclose with your manuscript to each publisher. This special letter is called a query letter. You will need to read on so that you will be able to write the correct letter to entice a publisher to read and consider your submission.

Query Letter

What do you say in a query letter? Here is one composed by a very great author.

> Strictly speaking, the manuscript is not yet in a form to be submitted to you; nevertheless I venture to suggest that you should allow me to send you Part I, not, of course, for a decision or a promise of any kind, but only to give you a view of the subject and the treatment.
>
> If you would consent to look through it at your perfect leisure I would go on writing in the meantime . . .
>
> I would also, with the part 1st send you a short statement . . . of the idea . . . and this would enable you . . . to form an opinion as to whether I am going about it in a promising way—or otherwise . . .

The above was excerpted from a letter dated August 28, 1897, written by Joseph Conrad to Wm. Blackwood, publisher. Blackwood had already published some of Conrad's work, yet note how unassuming and tactful the letter is and how Conrad shies away from presumptuousness. Conrad's letter included the essentials of a query letter. Of course, one would probably not write such a letter today. Editors usually prefer a simple, direct query presenting the idea or subject of the work in one or two sentences, citing the author's background, previous publications if any, and special qualifications for the chosen subject. Your query might read as follows:

Dear Ms. Pickins:

I have just completed an article entitled "The Sound of Street Music," which I thought might be suitable for *Westcoast Music* magazine. My article depicts the unusual lifestyle of California street musicians, their social and educational backgrounds, and their characters.

It explores their motivations, frustrations, and hopes for the future. I can submit a number of excellent photographs with my manuscript.

[Follow with your educational and professional background and qualifications: for example, editor of your high school literary magazine, reporter for your college daily newspaper, minor in music in college, and so forth.]

Would you be interested in considering this article for *Westcoast Music* magazine?

Sincerely,

Letter of Proposal

An alternative approach is to send a letter suggesting that you would like to do an article (or book) on a particular subject on which you have done research or in which you have had experience. In this case, you may wish to enclose an outline of the proposed work along with a brief sample—two or three typed pages for an article, a single chapter for a book.

Final Appraisal

Before you put your manuscript in the mailbox, check it over again. Keep these questions in mind as you make your final review:

- Is my article properly slanted to meet the needs of the magazine?

- Does it conform in style, subject, length, and slant to the magazine's specific requirements?
- Am I satisfied that my manuscript is sharply focused, vivid, and intriguing enough to hold the reader's interest?
- Is it in perfect shape—neat, unsmudged, clearly legible?
- Have I double-checked it for typing errors, grammar, punctuation, and spelling?
- Are its paragraphs carefully composed units—one topic sentence each, clarified by related sentences?
- Is each paragraph linked logically and smoothly to its successor?
- If my manuscript is rejected, have I the confidence to continue my marketing search with another query letter, rewriting the article if necessary to fit new specifications?

If you can answer yes to these questions, your manuscript is ready for an editorial reading. Mail it.

Establishing a Freelance Career

When a full-time freelancer stops working, he or she stops earning. Once a business-minded freelance writer has posted the query letter, he or she will immediately begin work on another article, for the writer will need to have more than one or two manuscripts in the mail at all times. For the novice this may be an improbable achievement. The economic stress alone might be self-defeating. A part-time job will serve to ease the writer into a freelance career.

Should Ms. Pickins's response be a positive one, you will, in due time, become a published professional freelance writer, and on publication you will have a title and a periodical name to refer to in ensuing queries. And, we hope, another and another. Thus not only the imaginary Ms. Pickins, but also other real-life editors will begin to recognize your name as a qualified, reliable writer. From that point on it is plausible to begin asking to write "on assignment," in which case you need only query the editor on an idea, not a completed work. However, for the time being you will be writing "on speculation," and this means with no promises. When you can produce articles of a style and literary quality suitable for the national magazine market, instead of $250 per article you may be earning $200 per page.

Suggested Reading

Bowling, Anne (Editor). *2005 Novel & Short Story Writer's Market.* F & W Publications, 2004.

Brogan, Kathryn. *2005 Writer's Market.* F & W Publications, 2004.

Bykofsky, Sheree. *The Complete Idiot's Guide to Getting Published.* Alpha, 2003.

Curtis, Richard. *How to Be Your Own Literary Agent: An Insider's Guide to Getting Your Book Published.* Houghton Mifflin, 2003.

Deval, Jacqueline. *Publicize Your Book! An Insider's Guide to Getting Your Book the Attention It Deserves.* Penguin, 2003.

Hupalo, Peter I. *How to Start and Run a Small Book Publishing Company: A Small Business Guide to Self-Publishing and Independent Publishing.* HCM Publishing, 2002.

Lee, Betsy B. *A Basic Guide to Writing, Selling, and Promoting Children's Books: Plus Information About Self-Publishing.* Learning Abilities Books, 2000.

Poynter, Dan. *Self-Publishing Manual: How to Write, Print, and Sell Your Own Book*. Para Publishing, 2003.

Warren, Lissa. *The Savvy Author's Guide to Book Publicity: A Comprehensive Resource: From Building the Buzz to Pitching the Press*. Avalon Publishing, 2004.

Appendix

Writers' Organizations and Associations

Academy of American Poets
584 Broadway, Ste. 604
New York, NY 10112-5243
www.poets.org

American Society of Journalists and Authors
1501 Broadway, Ste. 302
New York, NY 10036
www.asja.org

Associated Business Writers of America
1450 S. Havana, Ste. 620
Aurora, CO 80012

Dramatists Guild of America
1501 Broadway, Ste. 701
New York, NY 10036
www.dramaguild.com

Feminists Writers' Guild
P.O. Box 14055
Chicago, IL 60647-4301

Mystery Writers of America
17 E. 47th St., 6th Fl.
New York, NY 10017
www.mysterywriters.org

Science Fiction and Fantasy Writers of America, Inc.
P.O. Box 877
Chestertown, MD 21620
www.sfwa.org

Writers Guild of America, East
555 W. 57th St., Ste. 1230
New York, NY 10019
www.wgaeast.org

Writers Guild of America, West
700 W. Third St.
Los Angeles, CA 90048
www.wga.org

Associations with Career Information

Accrediting Council on Education in Journalism and Mass
    Communications
Stauffer-Flint Hall
1435 Jayhawk Blvd.
Lawrence, KS 66045-7575

American Advertising Federation
1101 Vermont Ave. NW, Ste. 500
Washington, DC 20005-6306
www.aaf.org

American Association of Advertising Agencies
405 Lexington Ave., 18th Fl.
New York, NY 10174-1801
www.aaaa.org

American Booksellers Association
828 S. Broadway
Tarrytown, NY 10591
www.bookweb.org

Association of American Publishers
50 F St. NW, Ste. 400
Washington, DC 20001
or
71 Fifth Ave., 2nd Fl.
New York, NY 10003
www.publishers.org

Association for Education in Journalism and Mass Communication
College of Journalism
234 Outlet Point Blvd.
University of South Carolina
Columbia, SC 29210
www.aejmc.org

Association for Women in Communications
780 Ritchie Hwy., Ste. 28-S
Severna Park, MD 21146
www.womcom.org

Business/Professional Advertising Association
205 E. Forty-Second St.
New York, NY 10017

Council for the Advancement of Science Writing
P.O. Box 910
Hedgesville, WV 25427
www.casw.org

Dow Jones Newspaper Fund
P.O. Box 300
Princeton, NJ 08543-0300
www.djnewspaperfund.dowjones.com

Magazine Publishers of America
810 Seventh Ave., 24th Fl.
New York, NY 10019
www.magazine.org

National Association of Science Writers
P.O. Box 890
Hedgesville, WV 25427
www.nasw.org

National Newspaper Publishers Association
3200 Thirteenth St. NW
Washington, DC 20010
www.nnpa.org

Public Relations Society of America
33 Maiden La., 11th Fl.
New York, NY 10038-5150
www.prsa.org

Society of Professional Journalists, Sigma Delta Chi
Eugene Pulliam National Journalism Center
3909 N. Meridian St.
Indianapolis, IN 46208
www.spj.org

Society for Technical Communication
901 N. Stuart St., Ste. 904
Arlington, VA 22203
www.stc.org

About the Author

Elizabeth Foote-Smith wrote her first piece of fiction at the age of ten. Although she continued over the years to write poetry, short stories, and plays "just for the pleasure and the challenge," years passed before she considered a professional writing career.

Instead, in response to a strong impulse toward music (and with a minor in music from the University of Minnesota), she became first a composer performing her own music, then a piano instructor, and finally a jazz pianist.

After receiving a bachelor's degree from Northwestern University and a master's degree from the University of Chicago in English Language and Literature, she spent five years teaching—English in suburban Illinois high schools, and literature and writing courses at the University of Wisconsin—where, finally, she determined to become a full-time writer.

Her publications include poetry, short stories, and three novels, two of them mysteries published by Putnam. *Opportunities in Writing Careers* is her first published nonfiction book.